D0467379

# The World's
# Worst Poetry

# The World's Worst Poetry

Stephen Robins

PRION

First published 2002 by
Prion Books Limited
Imperial Works, Perren Street
London NW5 3ED
www.prionbooks.com

ISBN 1-85375-481-1

A catalogue record of this book can be obtained from the
British Library

Jacket design by Carroll Associates
Printed and bound in Great Britain
by Creative Print & Design, south Wales

# CONTENTS

The following abbreviation appears in this work:
**fl.**    flourished

# INTRODUCTION

I would like to assure the reader at the outset that I love poetry. I tell you this so as not to be accused of knocking a noble art. To prevent this book from inspiring such accusations, I assure you that I do not intend to ridicule poetry. I do not even intend to ridicule bad poetry, for I love bad poetry as much as I love good poetry. This declaration is necessary because it is always very easy for the public to criticise the critic. The critic who praises the High Arts is accused of cultural elitism. The critic who sees value in popular arts is deemed a philistine. I fear that I may lay myself open to both charges, for the following pages include bad poems from both categories.

It is unfortunate that our foremost scholar of bad verse, Mr D. B. Wyndham Lewis, was something of a cultural elitist. He appreciated highbrow bad verse but had no time for lowbrow bad verse. The former he called 'Good Bad Verse'; the latter, 'Bad Bad Verse'. As he explained in 1930: 'Good Bad Verse is grammatical, it is constructed according to the Rubrics, its rhythms, rhymes, and metres are impeccable.' Bathos was the quality he rated most highly in Bad Verse:

'Bad Bad Verse is a strong but inexperienced female child doggedly attacking Debussy's *Fêtes* in a remote provincial suburb on a hire-payment pianoforte from the Swiftsure

Furnishing Stores. Good Bad Verse is Rummel or Lamond executing *Warblings at Eve* at Queen's Hall on a Bechstein concert-grand.'

I hope that the reading public of the twenty-first century has no truck with such snobbery, for I make no such distinction. Many of the poems in this collection are ungrammatical. Many of the rhymes are so forced as to be extremely amusing. Many of the verses – and one thinks in particular of those of William McGonagall – are little more than doggerel. One is reminded of the verse of the sixteenth-century poet John Skelton: 'rhymes ragged, / Tattered and jagged, / Rudely rain-beaten, / Rusty and moth eaten'. Samuel Taylor Coleridge defined good prose as 'words in their best order' and good poetry as 'the best words in the best order'. Much of the world's worst poetry can be characterised as the worst words in the worst order.

But there is more to bad poetry than bathos and technical incompetence. Sentimentality and banality make for awful verse, as is clear from the poems of Eliza Cook and Julia A. Moore. A complete absence of a sense of the ridiculous can be equally damaging, as seen in the verse of J. Gordon Coogler and Francis Saltus Saltus. Unintentional absurdity is a recurrent quality in the canon of bad verse. One thinks of Sir Richard Blackmore imagining herds of lowing cows flying through starry skies, or of John, Lord Hervey asking:

Or will the Mole her native earth forsake,
In wanton madness to explore the lake?

Naivety, excessive sincerity and moral admonition
combine to make the poems of Ella Wheeler Wilcox very
bad indeed. Self-importance and pretentiousness have
often been the cause of terrible poetry, and never more
so than in the case of Alfred Austin. John Keats said that
good poems come out naturally, whereas bad poems
must be forced out. I call this the theory of poetic
constipation, but Keats had a more agreeable metaphor:
'If poetry comes not as naturally as the leaves to a tree,'
he wrote, 'it had better not come at all'. One is put in
mind of Joyce Kilmer's line:

I think that I shall never see
A poem lovely as a tree.

The choice of subject matter is often very revealing. A
terrible topic will often indicate that a terrible poem will
ensue. Edward Newman wrote poems about insects.
James McIntyre wrote about cheese. William Tappan
praised tomatoes, and James Milligan celebrated geology
in verse. This book includes poems by James Grainger on
sugar cane, by John Dyer on sheep, and by Samuel Wesley
on maggots, pigs, and dead ducks. Inappropriate topics

are all too frequent. The reader receives medical advice from John Armstrong in 'The Art of Preserving Health'. Solyman Brown expounded on the theme of dentistry and dental hygiene in 'The Dentologia'. George Everleigh explored fiscal policy in 'Science Revealed'. To use the words of Alexander Pope, this is not poetry, but prose run mad.

Deaths of local infants provided suitable topics for Julia A. Moore, as seen in her poem 'Little Henry'. Disasters were often recorded in verse with disastrous results. The following pages include J. Stanyan Bigg on the Hartley Pit catastrophe, William McGonagall on the Albion battleship calamity, and Julia A. Moore on the Ashtabula disaster and the Chicago fire.

Sir Walter Scott saw the poet as the obsequious worshipper of Mute Nature, but in the nineteenth century the poet was more often the obsequious worshipper of Noisy Railways. The 'Railway Poets' are represented here by William Francis and by T. Baker with poems entitled 'The Steam Engine', by Sir William Allen with a poem called 'Thoughts on Steam', by Edward Dalton with 'The Railway Journey', and by the American Thomas Holley Chivers with his 'Railroad Song'.

The bad poet is often trapped by his milieu. He is a product of his age. He talks about commonplace things. He spouts the same truisms as other platitudinous men. He cannot escape from his surroundings. His verse is never timeless; thus the Railway Poets. The first half of the nineteenth century was the great age of rail. In 1836 and 1837, over 1,000 miles were added to British railroads. A second big boom came in the mid 1840s, and by 1848 some 5,000 miles of railways were working in the United Kingdom. Bad poets during this period, lacking imagination, versified on the themes of rail and steam.

It is no coincidence, however, that the nineteenth century produced some of the worst poetry ever seen. Industrialisation swelled the ranks of middle classes. An increase in literacy combined with eager religiosity and a renewed emphasis on moral conscience. The growth of the Empire created an appetite for all things patriotic, as seen, for example, in the poems of Martin Tupper or Eliza Cook on Englishmen.

The industrial and commercial classes, as a result of their wealth and increasing economic importance, came to dominate English society and culture after the middle decades of the nineteenth century. It is undeniable that they stamped on English development an impress peculiarly their own. These church-going, materialistic, educated and bombastic middle classes saw 'culture' as a duty. They wrote poems as a hobby. The work of Cornelius Whur, I fear, is more representative of mid-Victorian sentiment that we had hitherto feared.

S. J. R. London, 2002

# Sir William ALLEN
## (fl. 1870s)

It is much to be regretted that steam no longer excites the masses. Few people today seem ever to direct their minds to steam except when making tea or stepping into a sauna. We have, I fear, become bored by it. But steam has not always been neglected. In the nineteenth century, steam excited all but the most mild-tempered of individuals. Steam, it was widely believed, was the power behind the British Empire. It was a progressive and mighty force for good.

In his notable epic poem on steam, Sir William Allen developed the notion that steam was a resolutely Christian phenomenon. Rail networks, he predicted, would prove to be invaluable as a method of forcing Christianity on the tribesmen of various 'darkened' foreign lands. He envisaged that the 'dusky natives' would cast away their idolatrous beliefs the very moment that they cast their eyes on a train. Thus would 'heathenism' be confounded. Such a progressive policies much befitted a man who served as Member of Parliament for Gateshead for ten years.

John Armstrong

*From* **Thoughts on Steam**

Down with the rails! remotest clime surround,
The earth encompass with our iron bands;
The whistle's scream will heathenism confound,
Sole missionary best, for darkened lands,
And caste destroyed with no armed commands.
Deep in the forest, 'mid their rude abodes,
The dusky natives view with clasped hands
The harbinger of peace, with living loads,
And deem the white man's pow'r far greater than
                                            their gods.

# John ARMSTRONG
# (1709–1779)

It has been said that John Armstrong was
'spectacularly ungifted as a poet'. Little needs to be
added to this concise and accurate appraisal of his
ability. Armstrong, a dour Scottish physician, wrote
poems about medical matters. The extracts below are
taken from 'The Art of Preserving Health'.

In the first extract, Armstrong advises the reader on
the matter of diet. The wise man, says Armstrong, will
avoid 'the pure / Delicious fat, and all the race of oil'.
The jovial man, who only too readily imbibes these

**19**

gummy nutrients, should choose leaner viands. The verse is notable from the poet's description of Cheshire cheese as 'that which Cestria sends, tenacious paste / Of solid milk'. The second extract sees Armstrong advising his readers to wash in moderation ('just enough to keep / The body sacred from indecent soil') in order to improve their sex lives.

Armstrong, it seems, alienated people through his readiness to distribute unwanted advice. People became annoyed, and Armstrong came to despise them in return for their ingratitude. One contemporary said that Armstrong had 'a rooted aversion against the whole human race, except a few Friends, which it seems are dead'. Armstrong continued, however, in his study of disease, writing a prose work entitled *A Synopsis of the History and Cure of Venereal Diseases*. It is a rewarding read, but it does not surpass his poetry as a source of amusement.

### *From* The Art of Preserving Health

I

Nothing so foreign but th' athletic hind
Can labour into blood. The hungry meal
Alone he fears, or ailments too thin;
By violent powers too easily subdued,

Too soon expelled. His daily labour thaws,
To friendly chyle, the most rebellious mass
That salt can harden, or the smoke of years;
Nor does his gorge the luscious bacon rue,
Nor that which Cestria sends, tenacious paste
Of solid milk. But ye of softer clay,
Infirm and delicate! and ye who waste
With pale and bloated sloth the tedious day!
Avoid the stubborn aliment, avoid
The full repast; and let sagacious age
Grow wiser, lesson'd by the dropping teeth ...

The languid stomach curses even the pure
Delicious fat, and all the race of oil:
For more oily ailments relax
Its feebler tone; and with the eager lymph
(Fond to incorporate with all its meets)
Coyly they mix, and sun with slippery wiles
The woo'd embrace. The irresoluble oil,
So gentle late and blandishing, in floods
Of rancid bile o'erflows: what tumults hence,
What horrors rise, were nauseous to relate.
Choose leaner viands, ye whose jovial make
Too fast the gummy nutrient imbibes ...

There are, whose blood
Impetuous rages through the turgid veins,

Who better bear the fiery fruits of Ind
Than the moist melon, or pale cucumber.
Of chilly nature others fly the board
Supplied with slaughter, and the vernal powers
For cooler, kinder, sustenance implore.
Some even the generous nutriment detest
Which, in the shell, the sleeping embryo rears.
Some, more unhappy still, repent the gifts
Of Pales; soft, delicious and benign ...

The stomach, urged beyond its active tone,
Hardly to nutrimental chyle subdues
The softest food: unfinished and deprave,
The chyle, in all its future wand'rings, owns
Its turbid fountain; not by purer streams
So to be cleared, but foulness will remain ...

II

Against the rigours of a damp cold heaven
To fortify their bodies, some frequent
The gelid cistern; and, where nature forbids,
I praise their dauntless heart ...
Let those who from the frozen Arctos reach
Parched Mauritania, or the sultry West,
Or the wide flood that laves rich Indostan,
Plunge thrice a day, and in the tepid wave

Untwist their stubborn pores: that full and free
Th' evaporation through the softened skin
May bear proportion to the swelling blood.
So may they 'scape the fever's rapid flames;
So feel untainted the hot breath of hell.
With us, the man of no complaint demands
The warm ablution just enough to keep
The body sacred from indecent soil.
Still to be pure, even did it not conduce
(As much it does) to health, were greatly worth
Your daily pains. 'Tis this adorns the rich;
The want of this is poverty's worst woe;
With this external virtue age maintains
A decent grace; without it, youth and charms
Are loathsome. This the venal Graces know;
So doubtless do your wives: for married sires,
As well as lovers, still pretend to taste;
Nor is it less (all prudent wives can tell)
To lose a husband's than a lover's heart.

# Alfred AUSTIN
# (1835–1913)

Alfred Austin was undoubtedly the worst and most incompetent Poet Laureate ever to have held that position. Austin's supporters may disagree, saying that other Poets Laureate have written some pretty terrible stuff too. Certainly, every Poet Laureate has produced the occasional work of questionable merit. Cecil Day Lewis's 'Hail Teesside!' and Sir John Betjeman's poem on the Queen Mother's eightieth birthday immediately spring to mind. But whilst other Poets Laureate brought out the occasional bad verse, Austin never produced a good one.

It has been said that pretentiousness and incompetence were the main components of his work. This was apparent from the outset. 'Whether this, my first dash into the lists of public opinion, bring me plaudits or discomfiture,' he wrote in the Preface to his anonymously published first work in 1854, 'it will always mortify me that I was forbidden the chivalry of heralding my name. I must not raise my visor, unknown knight though I be.' The work was entitled *Randolph*. It sold 17 copies.

The defects of his style can be seen clearly in his notorious poem 'Go Away Death':

# Alfred Austin

Go away Death!
You have come too soon
To sunshine and song I but just awaken,
And the dew on my heart is undried and unshaken;
Come back at noon.

Austin was the compromise candidate for the
Laureateship. Until Lord Salisbury appointed him,
Austin worked as a conservative leader writer on *The
Standard*. He was not famous for his verse; indeed, it was
hardly known at all. 'The report that Alfred Austin was
to be Lord Tennyson's successor in the laureateship has
been confirmed,' wrote an anonymous journalist. 'Mr
Austin has been a prolific writer, but at 60 he has made
but little reputation as a poet. One thing, however, he has
in common with his predecessor: his Christian name.
Tennyson has occasionally been called Alfred the Great.
He will be called so oftener hereafter.'

Austin, of course, did not see it that way. 'Austin
himself used to say that his appointment was a very
simple matter,' wrote one contemporary, 'the recognition
of his being at the head of English literature.' The
critics, however, poured scorn on him. He was
lampooned in the satirical press. This has led to the
creation of two myths about Austin, both of which must
be put to rest. Firstly, Austin did not write of the illness
of the Prince of Wales:

> Along the wires the electric message came
> He is no better; he is much the same.

This was most probably written as a parody of Austin's work by one of his many detractors. Alternatively, it may have been taken from an entry in Oxford's Newdigate Prize Poem competition in 1871, the subject for which was 'The Prince of Wales's Illness'. Secondly, Austin did not write of the Jameson raid:

> They rode across the veldt
> As fast as they could pelt.

There is a grain of truth in this last myth, however, for Austin did write a poem about the Jameson raid in 1896, which was published in *The Times*. It included the lines:

> So we forded and galloped forward,
> As hard as our beasts could pelt,
> First eastward, then trending northward,
> Right over the rolling veldt.

I will go no further in defending Austin's reputation. I fear that little can be salvaged. It is already beyond repair. The first extract contains a memorable overblown Austinism in the last two lines.

# Alfred Austin

## *From* The Wind Speaks

The flocks of wandering waves I hold
In the hollows of my hand,
And I let them loose, like a huddled fold,
And with them I flood the land.

Till they swirl round villages, hamlets, thorpes,
As the cottagers flee for life:
Then I fling the fisherman's flaccid corpse
At the feet of the fisherman's wife.

## *From* Mozart's Grave

Where lies Mozart? Tradition shows
A likely spot: so much, no more:
No words of his own time disclose
When crossed he to the Further Shore,
Though later ages, roused to shame,
On tardy tomb have carved his name.

## *From* Is Life Worth Living?

Is life worth living? Yes, so long
As there is wrong to right,
Wail of the weak against the strong,

Or tyranny to fight;
So long as English songs are sung
Wherever blows the wind,
And England's laws and England's tongue
Enfranchise half mankind;
So long as in this ocean Realm,
Victoria and her Line
Retain the heritage of the helm,
By loyalty divine;
So long as flashes English steel,
And English trumpets shrill,
He is dead already who doth not feel
Life is worth living still.

## T. BAKER
## (fl. 1850s)

As has been noted already, the poets of the nineteenth century often expressed a fervent admiration of steam. Mr T. Baker was one of the more prodigious 'Steam Poets'. In 1857 he published 'The Steam Engine; or, the Power of Flame, and Original Poem, in Ten Cantos', a poem over two hundred pages in length. He states in his preface that the poem 'not only refers to the great achievements of the Flame-Powers, but also to the

almost divine aspirations of their Foster-Shires; who, in
a truly Christian spirit, sought to aggrandise and elevate
the human race'.

It is a cause of woe that so little is known about the
talented Mr T. Baker. The details of his life have been
lost in the mists of time. We do not even know what
Christian name lurks behind that mysterious initial. Even
the most pre-eminent scholars of bad poetry have
despaired. Messrs. Lewis and Lee in *The Stuffed Owl* wrote
that 'little or no discovery has rewarded diligent research
into the career of 'T'. Baker, except that he was
inexhaustibly impressed by the powers of steam.'

The first extract below records Lord Stanhope's
attempts to dabble in the tricky business of locomotive
engineering, which, as the poem reveals, were doomed
not to succeed. It has been pointed out by others that the
fourth line should not be read as suggesting that Lord
Stanhope's frame was made to emulate a duck; rather the
frame referred to was that of the amphibious craft under
consideration, namely, the duck-like frame of the duck
itself. I hope that makes things a little clearer. The
second extract records in verse the death of the politician
William Huskisson, who was run over by a train and
killed at the grand opening of a new railway line. The
fatality, it seems, did not hinder the day's joyful
celebrations too much.

# The World's Worst Poetry

*From* The Steam Engine

## I

Lord Stanhope hit upon a novel plan
Of bringing forth this vast Leviathan
(This notion first Genevois' genius struck);
His frame was made to emulate a duck;
Webb'd feet had he, in Ocean's brine to play;
With whale-like might he whirl'd aloft the spray;
But made with all this splash but little speed;
Alas! the duck was doomed not to succeed!

## II

The trains are stopp'd, the mighty chiefs of flame
To quench their thirst the crystal waters claim;
While from their post the great in crowds alight,
When, by a line-train, in its hasty flight,
Through striving to avoid it, Huskisson
By unforeseen mischance was over-run.
That stroke, alas! was death in shortest time;
Thus fell the great financier in his prime!
This fatal chance not only caused delay,
But damped the joy that erst had crown'd the day.

At length the Steam-Chiefs with replenish'd force
To Manchester pursued their pageant course;
A grand reception there secure they found;
And though acclaim still made the air resound,
The blithe response was clogg'd with grief's alloy,
The fate of Huskisson still chill'd their joy.
The mutual greetings and the banquet o'er,
The Steam-Chiefs, in procession as before,
With equal pomp and eight-fold gorgeous train,
Forthwith returned to Liverpool again:
While still the eager crowds, we scarce need say,
Their progress hail'd with plaudits all the way.
Now in conclusion, 'twould be vain to tell,
How high at Liverpool was rapture's swell!
How rich the banquet and how choice the wines,
Where thus in state the mighty Arthur dines!
While eloquence, like occasion, rare,
May be inferr'd, since Peel and Brougham were there!

# George BARLOW
## (fl. 1880s)

In 1880, George Barlow published a collection of poems
called *Love Songs*. The poem below, taken from that
collection, is an attempt to describe the realms of the
dead. With the benefit of hindsight, we can surmise how

such a terrible poem came to be written. Imagine, if you will, George Barlow at the end of a long day. He has been writing love poems since breakfast. He is sick to the back teeth of pretty little verses. He decides to pen a gruesome poem instead. He tries to imagine the most hideous and repugnant aspects of life beyond the grave. He experiences, however, a total and utter failure of his powers of imagination. The reader is left with the peculiar notion that dead men are content to smear doves' wings with clay whilst singing to a troupe of frolicking beetles.

### The Dead Men's Song

Praise we death
Who stays our breath
And sends us rest from pain;
Slay we life
With edge of knife
And hurl him back again.

Praise the tomb,
The utmost gloom
Of garments graveyards hold;
The dead man's lyre,
And flames of fire
From mouth of skeleton rolled.

# George Barlow

Praise the dance
Of feet that prance
Upon the ball-room floor
Deep down below,
Where worm-buds grow,
And light's alive no more.

Slay we love,
The feeble dove,
And smear her wings with clay!
Here below
We dead men know
Her not – the beetles play.

And mosses damp,
And clink of clamp,
And spiders' webs entwined
In hair of ours,
In woven bowers,
Are dear to dead men's mind.

Half-eaten eyes
With no surprise
We see: that sort of thing
Is common here;
Whole eyes are dear;
This is the song we sing.

The last stanza is more reminiscent of old ladies' gossip than of the laments of the dead. It sounds more like a complaint about rationing than a scene from a horror story. I believe that it can be rendered more convincingly in dialogue than in verse. The following conversation must be imagined as taking place in an old-fashioned café somewhere beyond the grave.

'You'll never guess what I saw yesterday,' said Doris, indignantly.

'What's that?' asked Edith, nibbling at her slice of ginger cake.

'I saw another half-eaten eye.'

'That's a shame,' said Edith, as placid as ever, 'but I'm not surprised. That sort of thing is increasingly common here.'

'Don't remind me,' snapped Doris. 'Whole eyes are dear these days.'

## Samuel BENTLEY
## (fl. 1760s)

The following poem is taken from a collection called *The River Dove*, which was written by Samuel Bentley in 1768. It concerns the death of Dean Langton. The tale is told with admirable clarity in the poem itself, but Bentley was evidently concerned that his readers would be too dim-witted to understand the poem itself, so he added a foot-note by way of elucidation. One critic has called the Dean's death 'one of the least moving in literature.' I am tempted to agree.

## A Fatal Frolic

Yet here, tho' amusing the Sight,
With Tears the poor Dean* I will mourn;
Who climb'd up this steep, dizzy Height,
By Ways he cou'd never return:
Ah! why did you ride up so high?
From whence all unheard sing the Birds,
Conduct a Fair Lady: Ah, why!
Where scarce is a Path for the Herds?

How shriek'd the hoarse Ravens a Knell!
When vain, and quite useless the Rein,
All headlong together down fell,
The Horse, the poor Lady, the Dean:
The Lady, by lace-braided Hair
Entangl'd in Brambles was found,
Suspended unhurt in mid-air;
The Dean met his Death with the Ground.

* The Reverend Dean Langton and Miss La Roache, who were on a visit to Wenman Cokes, Esq., at Longford, and went to entertain themselves with a sight of Dovedale, where the Dean was killed attempting to reach the top of one of the rocks, with the lady on the same horse; the lady was saved by her hair being entangled in some bushes.

# J. Stanyan BIGG
# (fl. 1840s–1860s)

J. Stanyan Bigg chose as his first career that of a journalist. He joined the unfairly neglected *Ulverston Advertiser* and worked his way up the ladder of ambition, no doubt fighting off stiff competition, until in time he became the editor-in-chief. He later edited *Downshire Protestant*, another unjustly forgotten rag.

The fire of his literary ambition was not quenched by his heady success, and he decided to become a novelist. Not satisfied with that, and upon deciding that poetry was the highest art form known to man, he reinvented himself as a poet, publishing three collections of poetry before his death. *The Sea King* (1848) was followed by *Night and the Soul* (1854).

The poem on the next page is taken from *Shifting Scenes* (1862), which was prefaced by a long discussion attacking Matthew Arnold's theory of poetry. 'Poetry,' wrote Bigg, 'needs no interpreter.' This is certainly true of Bigg's plodding and obvious verse, as the reader will see. 'Genuine poetry,' he continued, 'has the quality of pleasing those to who it is addressed.' I will leave the reader to decide to what extent he would have been pleased had the following poem been addressed to him.

## Hartley Pit Catastrophe

(Written by J. Stanyan Bigg, and delivered by T. Town,
Esq., Ulverston, at the Concert held there February
11th, 1862, on behalf of those who are bereaved by
the accident.)

Death in the Palace; Death within the Cot,
Death in all ranks! 'Tis but the common lot;
He comes with stealthy steps, and in the night,
Taketh our cherished treasure from our sight;
He tracks our steps, through hamlet, tower, and town,
And, with sure instinct, he brings his victim down;
And smites the pauper as he smites the crown.
With pallid face he leaps into his car,
And flames out ruddy in the sweat of war;
He comes unto the cottage door and knocks,
And then, in spite of bars, and bolts, and locks,
Some one gets up and goes, and is not seen –
Only another hillock on the green
Of the Sabbatic churchyard; all is done,
And one more mortal shall not see the sun!

But seldom to a village doth he come,
Wringing all hearts, and hushing the hum
Of its glad voices. Seldom is he seen
Wrapping in shadow all the village green;

Seldom he enters in at every door,
And writes the fearful legend up — "No more,"
Over the mantel-piece, and on the floor.
No more a father's shadow on the wall;
No more a husband's step, a brother's call,
No more the ruddy child with sunny hair,
Coming into the house — a psalm and prayer.
No more the eager hand upon the door,
For father, husband, brother, are no more.

Thus it has been at Hartley. Every room
Of every cottage hath its special gloom,
Some one is missing — husband, father, son,
Shall fill their place no more. Their day is done;
And there is night, and woe, and wail, and gloom,
And saddest shadows fill up all the room
Of the dear lost ones, each one in his place;
Death hath washed white each bronzed and ruddy
face;
And so of all the dearest ties an end,
Of father, husband, brother, child, and friend:
Husbands have said their last "Good morn," and boys
Have set aside for ever childish toys,
And with the morning breeze upon their breath
Have gone into the mysteries of death,
Their mothers' pleading arms not heeding; so
Went the grey-headed, so the strong men go

When the dread Angel makes the sign of woe.

A village has been stricken: On the door
Of every cottage are the words "No more;"
No more sturdy hands that won the bread,
Husband, and brother, child, and friend and dead.
And we, who come before you thus, tonight,
Cannot bring back the lost ones to the light;
Cannot refill the lorn and empty chair,
Cannot bring back the earnest evening prayer;
Cannot unto the mother give her son,
Nor to the wife her husband – all is done!
But still, amid this holocaust of dead,
The living need what we can give them – Bread!

# Sir Richard BLACKMORE
# (d. 1729)

In 1729 Richard Blackmore lay on his deathbed, considering, no doubt, posterity. How, he must have wondered, would future generations think of him? The answer, I regret to say, is that future generations haven't really thought of him at all. His works have been forgotten. I am of the opinion that this is unfair. Blackmore must be remembered by the public and receive at last such portion of acclaim as is deemed appropriate.

His first work, a study of the life of the legendary King Arthur, took the format of 'an heroick poem in ten books'. It had been composed, he said, 'for the greater part in coffee-houses, or in passing up and down the streets'. This hurried and rather haphazard method of composition had done little to improve the shape or consistency of the work, but Blackmore had found, or so he thought, his metier. He stuck to the formula, writing an epic poem in ten books about Queen Elizabeth and an epic poem in twelve books about King Alfred. He also wrote a prose work called *A Critical Dissertation on the Spleen*. His works must have been met with approval in some quarters, for he was knighted by William III in 1697.

The extracts below typify Blackmore's style, which is, in a word, quirky. In his poem on the creation of the world, he contemplates 'the wide womb of possibility' wherein lie 'many things, which ne'er may actual be'. Were things not as they are, the poet speculates, 'lowing herds' might 'break from the starry skies'. Lions, meanwhile, might have spots, whilst leopards might be entirely deprived thereof. It is left for the reader to infer that pigs might fly.

## Sir Richard Blackmore

*From* **The Book of Job**

With teats distended with their milky store,
Such num'rous lowing herds, before my door,
Their painful burden to unload did meet,
That we with butter might have wash'd our feet.


*From* **The Creation**

From Book III

If causal concourse did the world compose,
And things from hits fortuitous arose,
Than anything might come from anything;
For how from chance can constant order spring?
The forest oak might bear the blushing rose,
And fragrant myrtles thrive in Russian snows;
The fair pomegranate might adorn the pine,
The grape the bramble, and the sloe the vine;
Fish from the plains, birds from the floods, might rise,
And lowing herds break from the starry skies.

From Book V

In the wide womb of possibility
Lie many things, which ne'er may actual be;

And more productions, of a various kind,
Will cause no contradictions in the mind.
'Tis possible the things in Nature found,
Might different forms and different parts have own'd:
The bear might wear a trunk, the wolf a horn,
The peacock's train the bittern might adorn;
Strong tusks might in the horse's mouth have grown,
And lions might have spots, and leopards none.

# Solyman BROWN
# (1790–1876)

Solyman Brown was extremely active in the world of orthodontics. He ran a dental supplies outlet in Connecticut. He founded the American Society of Dental Surgeons. He formed the New York Teeth Manufacturing Company. Most impressively, however, he wrote poem on dentistry. Its full title is 'The Dentologia, A Poem on the Diseases of the Teeth and their Proper Remedies with Notes, Practical, Historical, Illustrative and Explanatory'. It runs to 54 pages.

At first it was serialised in *The American Journal of Dental Science*. It seems that Brown's fellow dentists enjoyed it, for it was published as a complete work in 1833, selling an impressive three hundred copies in advance of the

publication date. The most famous lines concern the
effect on a woman's lover of her blackened teeth:

> For when her parted lips disclosed to view,
> Those ruined arches, veiled in ebon hue,
> Where love had thought to feast the ravished sight
> On orient gems reflecting snowy light,
> Hope, disappointed, silently retired,
> Disgust triumphant came, and love expired!

'Dentists are frightening enough,' says one commenta-
tor, 'but dentists who write poetry are utterly terrifying.'

### From The Dentologia

> Whene'er along the ivory disks are seen,
> The rapid traces of the dark gangrene,
> When caries comes, with stealthy pace, to throw
> Corrosive ink-spots on those banks of snow,
> Brook no delay, ye trembling, suffering Fair,
> But fly for refuge to the Dentist's care.

> Whatever wealth and false refinement reign,
> The pampered appetites compose their train.
> Remotest climes supply the varied feast,
> But wisdom never comes it welcome guest
> The gormand-folly bids the poison pass,

And drains destruction from the circling glass.
The harmless flock, to cruel slaughter led,
Crowns high the board; for this the herd has bled,
For this, the gay musicians of the grove,
Suspend forever all their songs of love.
Earth, air, and ocean, each its part supplies
Of sentient life, to swell the sacrifice;
As though some fiend had sketched the darkest plan
Of bloody banquet for the monster-man!

But nature, sure to vindicate her cause,
Avenges each transgression of her laws.
Beware, rash man! for every nice offence,
Shall meet, in time a dreadful recompense;
Nor flight can save – nor necromantic art,
Nor dex'trous stratagem elude the smart –
For, lo, in fearful shapes, a haggard band
Of fell diseases wait at her command.

'Tis thus derangement, pain, and swift decay,
Obtain in man their desolating sway,
Corrupt his blood, infect his vital breath,
And urge him headlong to the shades of death.
No more his checks with flushing crimson glow;
No more he feels the sanguine current flow;
But quenched and dim his sightless eyeballs roll,
Nor meet one star that gilds the glowing pole!

## Solyman Brown

When first I saw her eyes, celestial blue,
Her cheeks vermilion, and the carmine hue,
That melted on her lips: her auburn hair
That floated playful on the yielding air;
And then that neck within those graceful curls,
Molten from Cleopatra's liquid pearls;
I whispered to my heart: we'll fondly seek
The means, the hour, to hear the angel speak;
For sure such language from those lips must flow,
As none but pure and seraph natures know.

'Twas said — 'twas done — the fit occasion came,
As if to quench betimes the kindling flame
Of love and admiration: for she spoke,
And lo, the heavenly spell forever broke,
The fancied angel vanished into air,
And left unfortunate Urilla there:
For when her parted lips disclosed to view,
Those ruined arches, veiled in ebon hue,
Where love had thought to feast the ravished sight
On orient gems reflecting snowy light,
Hope, disappointed, silently retired,
Disgust triumphant came, and love expired!

And yet, Urilla's single fault was small;
If by so harsh a name 'tis just to call

# The World's Worst Poetry

Her slight neglect: but 'tis with beauty's chain,
As 'tis with nature's: sunder it in twain
At any link, and you dissolve the whole,
As death disparts the body from the soul.

Yet, in that choir that sung the morning song,
One vacant seat afflicts the listening throng;
One well known voice, admired so oft before,
For sweetest melody, is heard no more.

Is Seraphina dead, whose melting strains
Had won the hearts of all the neighbouring swains?
Or does she now forsake the house of prayer,
And spurn her venerable pastor's care?
Unjust suspicion! tarnish not her fame,
Nor let reproach attaint her spotless name
For while her mellow voice obeyed her will,
She fondly lingered, our musician still;
And though by cruel fate compelled to part,
She leaves us all the homage of her heart,
To lonely solitude she gives her hours,
In shady copse, or shadier garden-bowers
In silent grief, and unconsoled she pines,
And scarce to heaven's high will her soul resigns.
For, lo, the heavenly music of her lip
So sweet, the labouring bees might stop to sip,
Has passed away discordant notes succeed,
And Seraphina's bosom lives to bleed.

Ye ask the cause: by premature decay,
Two of her dental pearls have passed away;
The two essential to those perfect strains,
That charm the soul when heavenly music reigns.
But fly, ye swains, to Seraphina fly,
And bid her fastly flowing tears be dry.
Haste to her cottage, where in vain she seeks
To wipe the burning deluge from her cheeks;
And when ye find her, sooth her frantic mind,
And bid her cast her sorrows to the wind;
In secret whisper this kind truth impart;
There is a remedy: the dental art
Can every varying tone with case restore,
And give thee music sweeter than before!

Thus, to desponding man, in life's dark way,
The angel, mercy points the opening day;
And through the tear that trembles in his eye,
Reveals the glories of her kindred sky.

# Samuel CARTER
## (fl. 1848)

In 1848 Samuel Carter was an ambitious young barrister. Unfortunately, no one wanted to give him any work. What could have remained a private and unannounced misfortune became a widely regretted tragedy, for Carter used this period of unwilling idleness to write some truly dreadful poetry.

His first and only volume of verse, *Midnight Effusions*, was published in 1848. It had been written, he said, 'at the dead of night, in the solitude of my own chamber'. It might have been better for the mental health of our nation if Carter and his poetry had remained locked in his chamber, but events proceeded otherwise and he unleashed his verses on the unlucky public.

The extract over the page describes London's 'magnificent' system of drains. Its 'sewers gigantic, like multiplied veins' are revealed in all their glory for the pleasure of the reader.

### *From* London

Magnificent, too, is the system of drains,
Exceeding the far-spoken wonders of old:
So lengthen'd and vast in its branches and chains,
That labyrinths pass like a tale that is old:

The sewers gigantic, like multiplied veins,
Beneath the whole city their windings unfold,
Disgorging the source of plagues, scourges, and pains,
Which visit those cities to cleanliness cold.
Well did the ancient proverb lay down this important
text,
That cleanliness for human weal to godliness is next.

# Margaret CAVENDISH, Duchess of Newcastle (1624–1674)

The diarist Samuel Pepys described the literary efforts of Margaret Cavendish, Duchess of Newcastle, as 'the most ridiculous thing that ever was wrote'. He called the woman herself 'mad, conceited and ridiculous'. The wife of the diarist John Evelyn dismissed the Duchess as 'airy, empty and ridiculous'.

The key word, it seems, was 'ridiculous'. She was ridiculous not simply because she wrote bad poetry, worse plays and — worst of all — philosophy. She was ridiculous because she took herself very seriously indeed. She was dim-witted and uneducated, but she thought very highly of her intellect and her learning. She was much given to pseudo-scientific theorising and devised more than a few interesting ideas, including the theory that longevity was linked to the density of atoms within the body. Messrs. Lewis and Lee recorded:

'It was her steady habit to dictate metaphysical and philosophical speculations at all hours, and the ladies attending her were compelled (according to Cibber) to sleep near at hand to her Grace in order that at the summons of her bell they might rise instantly an during the night to record in writing inspirations which might otherwise have been lost for ever.'

Margaret was born in Essex in 1623. She became a Maid of Honour to Queen Henrietta Maria. Whilst in Paris in 1645 she met William Cavendish, an ardent royalist living in exile during the Civil War. She married him the same year, and returned to England with him after the Restoration. She published *Poems and Fancies* in 1653. It was followed by many other works, including plays, letters and an informal biography of her husband. She was a genuine eccentric, as fantastic in her dress sense as in her writing. She had a predilection for face patches and clothed her footmen in velvet. She is buried in Westminster Abbey.

The first extract is from a longer poem in which the dotty Duchess tries to devise a suitable definition for water. The second poem is an excessively gruesome piece in which Cavendish expands a wholly inappropriate metaphor to the point of absurdity. It is amusing to think that this most self-important of women intended this rubbish to be taken seriously.

### *From* What is Liquid?

All that doth flow we cannot liquid name
Or else would fire and water be the same;
But that is liquid which is moist and wet;
Fire that property can never get:
Then 'tis not cold that doth the fire put out
But 'tis the wet that makes it die, no doubt.

### Nature's Cook

Death is the cook of Nature; and we find
Meat dressèd several ways to please her mind.
Some meats she roasts with fevers, burning hot,
And some she boils with dropsies in a pot.
Some for jelly consuming by degrees,
And some with ulcers, gravy out to squeeze.
Some flesh as sage she stuffs with gouts, and pains,
Others for tender meat hangs up in chains.
Some in the sea she pickles up to keep,
Others, as brawn is soused, those in wine steep.
Some with the pox, chops, flesh, and bones so small,
Of which she makes a French fricassee withal.

Some on gridirons of calentures is broiled,
And some is trodden on, and so quite spoiled.
But those are baked, when smothered they do die,
By hectic fevers some meat she doth fry.
In sweat sometimes she stews with savoury smell,
A hodge-podge of diseases tasteth well.
Brains dressed with apoplexy to Nature's wish,
Or swims with sauce of megrims in a dish.
And tongues she dries with smoke from stomachs ill,
Which as the second course she sends up still.
Then Death cuts throats, for blood-puddings to
make,
And puts them in the guts, which colics rack.
Some hunted are by Death, for deer that's red.
Or stall-fed oxen, knockèd on the head.
Some for bacon by Death are singed, or scalt,
Then powdered up with phlegm, and rheum that's
salt.

# Thomas Holley CHIVERS
# (1807–1858)

Chivers studied medicine at Transylvania University,
Lexington, Kentucky, in 1830, but he seldom practised
medicine. Instead he became a poet, an inventor and a

painter. He is remembered primarily for launching a vituperative attack against Edgar Allen Poe, claiming that Poe was guilty of plagiarism.

As pointed out already in relation to Sir William Allen and Mr T. Baker, few nineteenth-century poets could resist the temptation to discuss in verse the most momentous development of their age – the coming of the railways. Chivers wrote the most annoying of these poems. It is irritating in the extreme. Chivers sounds like a hyperactive and badly behaved child. One can imagine him chanting the poem whilst leaping around and hiding behind pieces of furniture.

### *From* Railroad Song

Clatta, clatta, clatta, clatter,
Like the devil beating batter
Down below in iron platter –
Which subsides into a clanky,
And a clinky, and a clanky,
And a clinky, clanky, clanky,
And a clanky, clinky, clanky;
And the song that now I offer
For Apollo's Golden Coffer –
With the friendship that I proffer –
Is for Riding on a Rail.

# Samuel Taylor COLERIDGE
# (1772–1834)

Samuel Taylor Coleridge was born in Ottery St. Mary in 1772, the youngest of ten children. After the death of his father, his brother Luke and his only sister Ann, he began to take laudanum, thus beginning his lifelong opium addiction. He went to Cambridge in 1791. In spite of the income received from some scholarships, he was a tad hard up and rapidly worked himself into debt with opium, alcohol, and women.

It was at Cambridge that he met Robert Southey. Southey introduced him to William Wordsworth, with whom Coleridge collaborated on the famous *Lyrical Ballads*, which was published in 1798. Coleridge was at times a great poet; but even good poets can write bad poems on occasion. The following is one of Coleridge's worst.

### To a Young Ass, Its Mother Being Tethered Near It

Poor little foal of an oppressed race!
I love the languid patience of thy face:
And oft with gentle hand I give thee bread,
And clap thy ragged coat, and pat thy head.
But what thy dulled spirits hath dismayed,
That never thou dost sport along the glade?

And (most unlike the nature of things young)
That earthward still thy moveless head is hung?
Do thy prophetic fears anticipate,
Meek Child of Misery! thy future fate?
The starving meal, and all the thousand aches
"Which patient Merit of the Unworthy takes"?
Or is thy sad heart thrilled with filial pain
To see thy wretched mother's shortened chain?
And truly, very piteous is her lot —
Chained to a log within a narrow spot,
Where the close-eaten grass is scarcely seen,
While sweet around her waves the tempting green!
Poor Ass! they master should have learnt to show
Pity — best taught by fellowship of Woe!
For much I fear me that He lives like thee,
Half famished in a land of Luxury!
How askingly its footsteps hither bend!
It seems to say, "And have I then one friend?"
Innocent foal! thou poor despised forlorn!
I hail thee Brother — spite of the fool's scorn!
And fain would take thee with me, in the Dell
Of Peace and mild Equality to dwell,
Where Toil shall call the charmer Health his bride,
And Laughter tickle Plenty's ribless side!
How thou wouldst toss thy heels in gamesome play,
And frisk about, as lamb or kitten gay!
Yea! and more musically sweet to me

Thy dissonant harsh bray of joy would be,
Than warbled melodies that soothe to rest
The aching of pale Fashion's vacant breast!

## J. Gordon COOGLER
## (1865–1901)

J. Gordon Coogler worked in a printshop, the front
window of which carried a sign reading 'Poems Written
While You Wait'. His poems do read as if they were
written with extraordinary speed.

The following poem was reviewed by the magazine
*Puck* in 1894: 'Byron's mother may not have been an
admirable woman,' wrote the reviewer, 'and she may have
had the gravest of faults; but she died many years ago,
and we protest that J. Gordon Coogler has no right to
rake up any old scandal about her, especially in an ode to
her talented son.'

### Byron

Oh, thou immortal bard!
Men may condemn the song
That issued from thy heart sublime,
Yet alas! its music sweet
Has left an echo that will sound

Thro' the lone corridors of Time.

Thou immortal Byron!
Thy inspired genius
Let no man attempt to smother –
May all that was good within thee
Be attributed to Heaven,
All that was evil – to thy mother.

**From How Strange Are Dreams!**

How strange are dreams! I dreamed the other night
A dream that made me tremble,
Not with fear, but with a kind of strange reality,
My supper, though late, consisted of no cheese.


# Eliza COOK
# (1818–1889)

Eliza Cook began her literary efforts whilst a child and
contributed to magazines from an early age. Her first
noteworthy poem was called 'I'm Afloat!' In 1849 she
published *Eliza Cook's Journal*. It ceased to appear in 1854,
prompting one wit to write a satirical poem called 'I'm
Sunk!' But Cook bounced back, and much of her work was

regurgitated as *Jottings from my Journal* (1860).

Her poems can be compared with wholemeal bread in that they are heavy, fibre-rich and somewhat redolent of yeast. Homeliness, patriotism and an overbearing moral tone characterise her work.

## The Englishman

There's a land that bears a world-known name,
Though it is but a little spot;
I say 'tis first on the scroll of Fame,
And who shall say it is not?
Of the deathless ones who shine and live
In Arms, in Arts, or Song,
The brightest the whole wide world can give
To that little land belong.
'Tis the star of earth, deny it who can,
The island home of an Englishman.

There's a flag that waves o'er every sea,
No matter when or where;
And to treat that flag as aught but the free
Is more than the strongest dare.
For the lion-spirits that tread the deck
Have carried the palm of the brave;
And that flag may sink with a shot-torn wreck,
But never float over a slave.

Its honour is stainless, deny it who can;
And this is the flag of an Englishman.

There's a heart that leaps with burning glow,
The wronged and the weak to defend;
And strikes as soon for a trampled foe,
As it does for a soul-bound friend.
It nurtures a deep and honest love;
It glows with faith and pride;
And yearns with the fondness of a dove,
To the light of its own fireside.
'Tis a rich, rough gem, deny it who can;
And this is the heart of an Englishman.

The Briton may traverse the pole or the zone,
And boldly claim his right;
For he calls such a vast domain his own,
That the sun never sets on his might.
Let the haughty stranger seek to know
The place of his home and birth;
And a flush will pour from cheek to brow,
While he tells his native earth.
For a glorious charter, deny it who can,
Is breathed in the words, "I'm an Englishman."

*From* Song of the Sea Weed

Many a lip is gaping for a drink,
And madly calling for rain;
And some hot brains are beginning to think
Of a messmate's opened vein.

*From* A Temperance Song

Who shall talk of strength and freedom,
With a loud and fevered breath,
While they let a full cup lead 'em
To the slavery of death?

Men of labour, wake to thinking,
Shout not with a reeling brain!
Lips that argue o'er deep drinking
Ever yield more chaff than grain.

Do ye find the hot libation,
Poured so wildly on the heart,
Make it fitter for its station,
Whatsoe'er may be its part?

Who shall reckon all the anguish,
Who shall dream of all the sin,

Who shall tell the souls that languish
At the spectral-shrine of Gin?

Oh! stand back in godly terror,
When Temptation's joys begin;
'Tis such wily maze of Error,
Few get out who once go in.

# Thomas COSTLEY
# (fl. 1890s)

Here we are hindered by an annoying dearth of essential
biographical information. It is known that Thomas Costley
wrote and published a collection of verse called *Sketches of
Southport*. We can be certain that the book was published in
Manchester, for it says as much on the first page.

But we know little else. We do not even know the exact
date of publication. It has been estimated in some quar-
ters that it was published in 1895, but we can never be
certain. Most people, of course, are lucky enough not to
care about such matters.

Southport, says the poet, has no peer — provided, that
is, that all the beauty contained therein can be 'set forth
truly in descriptive phrase'. With this one proviso in
mind, the reader is invited to soak up the poetic beauties
of Southport's mudless streets.

## The Botanic Gardens, Churchtown

Southport, once desolate and void of fame,
Has now no peer, if all the beauty it contains
Is set forth truly in descriptive phrase.
Its streets are mudless after copious rains,
And dry before the clouds have passed away.
Each house is free from grime, and weather-stains.
But though the town itself is beautiful,
Its mansions noble, and its trees and bowers
Abundant, in its gardens and its streets;
It would be wanting if St Cuthbert's Church
At Churchtown did not speak of its antiquity;
Or if that ancient village was deprived
Of one supremely beautiful retreat
Where botany is not a book but life,
That loves before us in its majesty.
In the Botanic Gardens, floral wealth
Is too abundant to be told or spent;
Exotics flourish as if native-born,
Nor languish for the want of sun and home.
Fantastic walks bewilder and beguile,
Smooth lawns are here, and borders void of weeds.
Grapes in the vineries pleasant pictures make,
And wondering mouths gape all unconsciously.
Erections light, with roofs and walls of glass,
Keep tender blooms from frost and nightly dews.

And when the stranger is intoxicate
With too much pleasure, let him turn aside
To view the curious things that have no life,
In the Museum, worthy to be seen;
Say not that to Southport thou hast been
If thou the Churchtown Gardens hast not seen!

# George CRABBE
# (1754–1832)

Over 70 years ago, Messrs. Lewis and Lee described
Crabbe's verse in the following terms: 'not sloppy verse,
not wasty, pappy verse, not verse blanchified, but strong,
heavy, brown, bad verse.' They noted that this poem
marks the only appearance of the firm of Clutterbuck
and Co. in the history of English poetry.

### *From* Tales of the Hall: The Elder Brother

Something one day occurr'd about a bill
That was not drawn with true mercantile skill,
And I was ask'd and authorised to go
To seek the firm of Clutterbuck and Co.;
Their hour was past – but when I urg'd the case,
There was a youth who named a second place,
Where, on occasions of important kind,

I might the man of occupation find,
In his retirement, where he found repose
From the vexations that in Business rose.

The house was good, but not so pure and clean
As I had houses of retirement seen,
Yet men, I knew, of meditation deep,
Love not their maidens should their studies sweep.
His room I saw, and must acknowledge, there
Were not the signs of cleanliness or care:
A female servant, void of female grace,
Loose in attire, proceeded to the place;
She stared intrusive on my slender frame,
And boldly ask'd my business and my name.

I gave them both; and, left to be amused,
Well as I might, the parlour I perused ...
There were strange sights and scents about the room,
Of food high-season'd, and of strong perfume; ...

A large mirror, with once-gilded frame,
Reflected prints that I forbear to name –
Such as a youth might purchase – but, in truth,
Not a sedate or sober-minded youth.
The chairs in haste seem'd whirl'd about the room,
As when the sons of riot hurry home
And leave the troubled place to solitude and gloom.

# Lillian E. Curtis
# (fl. 1870s)

Lillian E. Curtis hailed from Chicago. One can almost feel the cruel wind of that city gusting through her bleak and windswept poetry. Her first collection, entitled *Forget-Me-Not*, contained miserable verse with titles such as 'We All Must Pass Away'. The following is one of her more cheerful poems.

### Only One Eye

Oh! she was a lovely girl,
So pretty and so fair,
With gentle, lovelit eyes,
And wavy, dark-brown hair.

I loved the gentle girl,
But oh! I heaved a sigh,
When first she told me she could see
Out of only one eye.

But soon I thought within myself,
I'd better save my tear and sigh,
To bestow upon some I know,
Who has more than one eye.

She is brave and intelligent,
Too she is witty and wise,
She'll accomplish more now, than many,
Who have two eyes.

Ah! you need not pity her,
She needs not your tear and sigh,
She makes good use, I tell you,
Of her one remaining eye.

In the home where we are hastening,
In our eternal Home on High,
See that you be not rivalled,
By the girl with only one eye.

# Edward DALTON
# (fl. 1870s)

The Reverend Edward Dalton wrote a collection of verse entitled *The Sea, The Railway Journey, and Other Poems*. It was published in the 1870s. The following poem is notable for the poet's tendency to jump to unlikely conclusions. For the most part, his deductions are as peculiar as they are improbable. Fortunately, however, he seems always to redeem himself by reconsidering his opinion and ascertaining eventually the correct answer. One can only conclude that Dalton was as deaf as he was alarmist.

*From* **The Railway Journey**

The last friends part,
And off we start,
The engine pants and snorts and blows,
The carriage doorways slam and close,
The broad and ponderous wheels are rolled
By thick-set arms of iron mould,
While streaming from the spouting side
The steam escapes in hissing tide.
Cranch, cranch, thud, rud, dubber-dub-rub,
Thudder, rubber dub-dub, dub-a-rub-rub-rub.

Startled at starting, for our nerves are weak,
We gasp for breath,
Grow pale as death,
As one long piercing, shrill, unearthly shriek
Rings thro' our ears, and stops the power to speak,
The cry of anguish, or vindictive yell,
Of baffled imp, or vanquished fiend of hell,
The death-shriek of monstrous beast,
We've smashed a million pigs at least.
Ah no! no suckling pig has lost a bristle,
The shriek was but the starting railway whistle.

Our speed increases as we rattle down
And reach the suburbs of the outer town;
And there, yes, there
On the look-our slope of the garden sward
I caught a glimpse of my darling Maude ...

Crash! crash! what's that? a peal of thunder?
A rattling volley? No, a bridge we've just passed under.

# Sidney DOBELL
# (1824–1874)

Sidney Dobell was a member of the 'Spasmodic School'. The nickname was given to Dobell and his associates by William Edmondstoune Aytoun, whose 'spasmodic tragedy' – a parody entitled *Firmilian* – ensured that the Spasmodics would never be taken seriously.

Shining like a bright star amidst the darkness of Dobell's other work is the poem printed below. 'Oh the wold,' says the poet, 'the wold!' Indeed, he makes 42 mentions of the wold in a mere 36 lines of verse. Also notable is the infamous line from 'Balder', in which the protagonist is made to say 'ah!' ten times in one line in order to keep to the strict decasyllabic metre.

## Wind

Oh the wold, the wold,
Oh the wold, the wold!
Oh the winter stark,
Oh the level dark,
On the wold, the wold, the wold!

Oh the wold, the wold,
Oh the wold, the wold!
Oh the mystery
Of the blasted tree
On the wold, the wold, the wold!

Oh the wold, the wold,
Oh the wold, the wold!
Oh the owlet's croon
To the haggard moon,
To the waning moon,
On the wold, the wold, the wold!

Oh the wold, the wold,
Oh the wold, the wold!
Oh the fleshless state,
Oh the windy hair,
On the wold, the wold, the wold!

Oh the wold, the wold,
Oh the wold, the wold!
Oh the cold sigh,
Oh the hollow cry,
The lean and hollow cry,
On the wold, the wold, the wold!

Oh the wold, the wold,
Oh the wold, the wold!
Oh the white sight,
Oh the shuddering night,
The shivering shuddering night,
On the wold, the wold, the wold!

*From* **Balder**

[Scene XXXVIII]

BALDER. It shall not be! Amy!
         [*Looking up, his eye catches the clouds.*]
         You white full heavens!
You crowded heavens that mine eyes left but now
Shining and void and azure!
                Ah! ah! ah!
Ah! ah! ah! ah! ah! ah! ah! ah! ah! ah!
By Satan! this is well. What! am I judged?

# Henry DOMAN
# (fl. 1860s)

Henry Doman was a printer and stationer at Lymington in Hampshire, in the years when Coventry Patmore lived in the town. Inspired by Patmore's success as a poet, Doman picked up the pen and called on the Muse for inspiration. The Muse must have been feeling particularly generous, for Doman wrote three volumes of verse. His first, *The Cathedral and Other Poems*, was published in 1864 and received a cautious welcome from the less reputable of critics. His second, *Songs of Lymington*, met with an indifferent public in 1867. Since Doman was a printer and his books were issued from his own press, the lack of acclaim was not fatal to his literary ambitions. His last book, *Songs in the Shade*, was largely ignored when it was published in 1881.

### The Street Funeral

Silently, solemnly,
Steadily go!
The dead above,
The living below.
Leisurely, measurely,
Footsteps are falling
Under the coffin;
The sound is appalling!

Weepingly, creepingly,
Sorrowful, dumb,
The chief of the mourners,
All desolate, come.
The friends and relations
By two and two follow;
And their tramp on the pavement
Sounds dreary and hollow.

The folks from their windows
Look out at the show,
At the pall of black velvet,
With fringes of snow –
At the style of the mourning,
Its fashion and shape –
The bugles and flounces,
The broadcloth and crape.

Silently, solemnly,
Steadily go!
The dead above,
The living below.
Leisurely, measurely,
Footsteps are falling
Under the coffin;
The sound is appalling!

# John DYER
# (1700–1757)

John Dyer was born in 1700. He spent the bulk of his adult life writing and polishing his masterpiece, an epic poem about sheep. Refined and perfected far beyond the ordinary scope of human achievement, it was published as 'The Fleece' in 1757. The poet, exhausted by the sheer effort of completing this grand epic, died days later.

Never before has a death been so well timed. Had he lived for a few months more, Dyer would no doubt have been crushed and disappointed to see the derisory response that greeted his work. The reading public, it seemed, was not especially interested in sheep. Those members of the public who were interested in sheep were not, by all accounts, avid readers of poetry.

I nurture a sincere hope that the mood has changed since 1757, and that the reading public has now developed an insatiable desire for sheep poetry. Animal welfare is now the priority of our most sagacious politicians. Animal rights can now be discussed without inspiring mirth in the listener. The bestseller lists hint at a widespread hunger to read about 'the diseases of the bleating kind'.

We learn, in the extracts that follow, that sheep gladly resign their wool to the hatter's use and that savage 'Hottentots' practise euthanasia. As you will realise, 'The Fleece' is an exciting poem. Its time has come. It will, I am certain, be neglected no longer.

*From* **The Fleece**
From Book I

In cold stiff soils the bleaters oft complain
Of gouty ails, by shepherds termed the halt:
Those let the neighbouring fold or ready crook
Detain: and pour into their cloven feet
Corrosive drugs, deep-searching arsenic,
Dry alum, verdigris, or vitriol keen.
But if the doubtful mischief scarce appears,
'Twill serve to shift them to a drier turf,
And salt again: th' utility of salt
Teach thy slow swains: redundant humours cold
Are the diseases of the bleating kind.

From Book II

Wild rove the flocks, no burdening fleece they bear,
In fervid climes: Nature gives naught in vain.
Carmenian wool on the broad tail alone
Resplendent swells, enormous in its growth:
As the sleek ram from green to green removes,
On aiding wheels his heavy pride he draws,
And glad resigns it to the hatter's use.

From Book IV

        Mon'motapa's coast
Is seldom visited; and the rough shore
Of Caffres, land of savage Hottentots,
Whose hands unnatural hasten to the grave
Their aged parents: what barbarity
And brutal ignorance, where social trade
Is held contemptible!

## George EVERLEIGH
## (fl. 1863)

In October 1863, a London review called *The Reader* published a notice of a work 'in the heroic metre'. The work, by George Everleigh, was entitled 'Science Revealed; a Poem, descriptive of the Works of Creation and the Truth of Scriptural Record'.

In the preface the poet declared that his intention was to break down the barriers between Religion and Science and prove thereby 'the words of Scripture to be verbatimly correct and elegantly concise'. This is a lofty ambition indeed. One immediately wonders whether such a theme is best suited to verse. Everleigh, it seems, had predicted this query, for he wrote, 'I have chosen poetic composition as that by which scope and force are most readily attained and perpetuated.'

The reader is left to judge whether Everleigh achieved his aim. Others have thought so. 'The rhythmic surge of the blank verse, its rich yet sober texture, the sonorous clang of the lines,' wrote Messrs. Lewis and Lee, 'are all admirable.'

In the preamble to the extract below, Everleigh has argued that if mankind is to deal in mercy like its Maker, men must be company promoters. He sets out a new fiscal policy for the government to adopt. It will, he thinks, be of benefit of corporations and improve the moral worth of all involved.

### *From* Science Revealed

If, then, the State will but assistance lend,
To give security to Companies,
The Public Companies with monied wings
Will fly like eagles to the scent of prey,
And every nook and corner of the world
Will find its Companies of men at work;
And, for the aid each Company receives,
Each Company could well afford to pay,
Out of its surplus revenues, the State;
Two-thirds of each will reimburse the State,
And hold one-third a bonus to account,
Which gives the State two-thirds for profit too,

And two to reimburse the one that's lost.
Thus, if a Government agrees to give,
Whenever Public Companies are formed,
To each a dividend – say, six per cent
Per annum for a fixed time,
And for security inspects accounts –
Then, of the profits which each yieldeth more
Than the same dividend of six per cent,
Two-thirds the Government itself shall claim,
The other third remaining to afford
The Company an extra dividend.

# Edward Edwin FOOT
# (1828–1880)

The following sketch of Edward Edwin Foot was writ-
ten in the early 1870s and published in an
interminable series of volumes called *Poets of the West*, in
which the poets of Devon and Cornwall were profiled.
This sketch has the benefit of being a contemporaneous
description of the poet written after the publication of
his only book of verse, *The Original Poems of Edward Edwin
Foot, of her Majesty's Customs, London*. It is the only source of
biographical information we have about Edward Edwin
Foot, and deserves, for its admirable detail, to be
reprinted here.

'Mr Edward Edwin Foot, from whom we have had some difficulty in procuring an account of himself – his modest reticence pleading very strongly to be excused from being immortalized among the 'Poets of the West' – was born at Ashburton, Devonshire, in 1828, where his father, the late Mr Peter Foot, carried on the business of a boot and shoe maker ... Edward seems to have had but a very indifferent amount of education at the Free School, simply acquiring reading, writing, and arithmetic; after trying his hand at several occupations (being always of a restless disposition), he eventually was apprenticed to the trade of a house-painter and glazier, of which he ultimately became a master tradesman.

'In the meantime, possessing rather an inventive genius, he, in the year 1854, designed and submitted to the War Office the drawing of a breech-loading man-of-war's gun, which received the careful attention of the authorities, by the direction of the Duke of Newcastle, but without success. Later on, during the Crimean campaign, he submitted to the Inspector-General of Fortifications plans and specifications of a military hut of his invention, executing the drawings to scale himself for which he was awarded the sum of £50. Again, in 1865, he forwarded to the Postmaster-General his design of a postal exchange stamp, which, although unsuccessful, no doubt, had something to do with the origin of the present postal order.

# Edward Edwin Foot

'In the year 1855 Mr Foot went to Australia, returning in 1857, shortly afterwards obtaining an appointment in Her Majesty's Customs, London, also following his musical instincts as a theatrical bandsman and a paid church-singer. We find him expressing great regret that his school education was so limited, as in after-years he had to educate himself.

'It appears that, although "dabbling", as he calls it, in verse at an early period of his life, it was only at the commencement of his London career that he turned his more earnest attention to the Muse, and made his first poetical adventure in sending a manuscript poem entitled "Evening" to Lord Palmerston, who a few days afterwards sent the author a sovereign in acknowledgement. This acted as a stimulant, causing him to devote more of his leisure time in that direction – sending various pieces to members of the Royal Family, receiving most gratifying letters in reply.

'In 1867 he resolved upon publishing a book of poems by subscription, and was successful in procuring five hundred and forty subscribers at 3s 6d per volume before going to press, which more than cleared the expense of the three thousand copies printed, leaving the remainder as profit. The Queen graciously accepted a copy of this book, and sent the author a present of £2. We should like to see another edition of Mr. Foot's poems, and the publication of other manuscripts which he has in hand; but it appears that the pension he is now receiving from the Government is insufficient to warrant his risking such an enterprise. He therefore now confines himself to Ashburton, contributing occasional pieces to the Totnes papers, which are much appreciated by the readers of those local journals, the *Totnes Times* and the *Western Guardian*.'

What this sketch fails to point out is the one remarkable characteristic of Foot's poetry, namely, the footnotes. As you will see from the extracts that follow, Foot the Footnoter added superfluous explanatory footnotes to his poems in order to ensure that no ambiguities would arise in the mind of the reader.

### Palmerston

Altho' we[1] mourn for one now gone,
And he – that grey-hair'd Palmerston,[2]
We will give God the praise,
For he, beyond the age of man,[3]
Eleven years had over-ran
Within two equal days.

[1] The nation.

[2] The Right Honourable Henry John Temple, Viscount Palmerston, K.G., G.C.B., etc. (the then Premier of the British Government), died at "Brockett Hall," Herts., at a quarter to eleven o'clock in the forenoon of Wednesday, 18th October, 1865, aged eighty-one years (all but two days), having been born on the 20th October, 1784. The above lines were written on the occasion of his death.

[3] Scriptural limitation.

# Edward Edwin Foot

## *From* Raven Rock

Some summer's day, upon that rock,[1]
A cliff, wherein the ravens flock,
List ye to the Dart,[2] below;
See the little rapids flow:
From that proud stream no discords rise;
No shipwrecks e'er bedim our eyes.
Oft have I[3] watched, thereon, its course,
(Astride the rock as 'twere a horse)
Singing o'er a favourite song,
Twice and thrice to make it long.

[1] Raven Rock is about five hundred feet above and near the banks of the River Dart; it is distant about two and a half miles from Ashburton, Devonshire, and bounded on the north side by Aswell Woods from which it is easily accessible.

[2] The Dart river whose source is in the forest of Dartmore, is most appropriately called the "English Rhine". The scenery in the locality of "Raven Rock" is very beautiful.

[3] The author of the poem.

## *From* The Homeward Bound Passenger Ship

The captain scans the ruffled zone,[1]
And heeds the wind's increasing scope;
He knows full well, and reckons on
His seamanship, but God's his hope ...

Look, look ye down the plumbless deep,
See,[2] if ye can, their lifeless forms!
Here laid, poor things! across  steep,
An infant in its mother's arms.

[1] A figurative expression, intended by the Author to signify the horizon.
[2] Imagine.


# William FRANCIS
# (fl. 1840s)

William Francis was one of the terrible 'Railway Poets'
of the nineteenth century. These men were obsessed with
the power of steam and the workings of locomotives,
both of which are unpromising subjects for versifying. In
the first extract, Francis explains how a steam engine
works. It is, he says, a bit like the circulation of blood in
the human body. In the second, he praises 'Immortalis'd
Watt!'

### From The Steam Engine

In order we follow the skill'd engineer,
At condensing work next his men will appear;
First the cistern is laid, then follows the pan,
Air-pump and receiver, in orderly plan,

William Francis

Eduction pipe to, all design'd to receive
Spent steam from the piston, the same to relieve;
For without such relief above and below,
No vacuum's form'd, and steam ceasing to flow,
The engine no longer her power can exert,
But self-balanced by steam, she stands quite inert,
How like is all this, though differing in name,
To the circulation of blood in our frame:
The boiler would seem a mere counterpart
Of the stomach in animals, and of the heart:
In these food concocted is turn'd into chyle,
And chyle into blood, freed from waste and from bile,
Blood arterial and veinous, by the processes
Unperceiv'd yet active in the recesses
Of the stomach and heart, aorta and lungs;
Theme befitting the faculty's pens and their tongues;
But in likeness to these we plainly may see
The steam-making boiler and piston agree;
Blood through arteries forc'd and return'd by veins,
Conveys vital strength and our life too sustains;
See the picture in steam, conductors and drains ...

Immortalis'd Watt! though by others achieved,
These thy honour proclaim from thee they received
Their impulse, and surely thy spirit now knows
What improvements are made, and enraptur'd glows
All thankful to Him who thy genius inspired

To see what perfection thy plans have acquir'd;
In steam machinery, the theme of the day,
Minds congenial to thine with triumph essay:
Thy genius fell on many abroad and at home,
But thy mantle has dropt and descended on Loam.
Farther on where the hill to the southward inclines,
The tourist arrives at the United Mines;
Here similar proofs of mechanical pow'r
Arrest the attention, beguiling the hour.

## Adam Lindsay GORDON (1833–1870)

Adam Lindsay Gordon went from Oxford to Australia in 1853 and joined the mounted police as a trooper. In 1865 he sat as a Member for Victoria in the House of Assembly. In 1867 he left politics and published his first volume of poems, *Sea Spray and Smoke Drift*. In 1870 he published *Bush Ballads* and committed suicide. For now, the bare biographical details of Adam Lindsay Gordon to suffice. To say more is unnecessary. Instead, I exhort the reader to consider the following extract. It has been taken from 'Wolf and Hound', a stirring adventure poem, in which a stray bullet flays the narrator's ear-tip.

*From* **Wolf and Hound**

Flash! flash! bang! bang! and we blazed away,
And the grey roof reddened and rang;
Flash! flash! and I felt his bullet flay
The tip of my ear. Flash! bang!
Bang! flash! And my pistol arm fell broke;
I struck with my left hand then –
Struck at a corpse through a cloud of smoke —
I had shot him dead in his den!

# James GRAINGER
# (1721–1767)

The poet James Grainger had the rare honour of being laughed at by Samuel Johnson. This episode has prolonged Grainger's fame beyond the realms of the foreseeable. None of his contemporaries would have imagined for one moment that Grainger would be remembered in the twenty-first century. His poetry was terrible. It received attention neither from his peers, nor the press, nor the public. But Johnson laughed at Grainger. He laughed very hard. And Boswell recorded the incident, ensuring that Grainger would be remembered for as long as his *Life of Johnson* was read.

The occasion for the mirth was the imminent publication of 'The Sugar Cane' in 1759. Grainger, a self-important and pompous man at the best of times, told everyone who cared to listen that his forthcoming work was a masterpiece. Dr Johnson was not convinced. Indeed, he was sceptical to the point of suspicion. 'What could he make of a sugar cane?' Johnson said to Boswell. 'One might as well write "The Parsley Bed, a Poem," or "The Cabbage Garden, a Poem".'

Grainger attended Johnson's house to give a reading of 'The Sugar Cane' to the gathered literati in advance of publication. Boswell records the explosion of mirth that greeted the line, 'Now, Muse, let us sing of rats!' Grainger, determined to explain the origin of the line, told his listeners that it had originally read, 'Now, Muse, let us sing of mice!' but that it had been changed to appear more dignified. Johnson laughed a great deal at this purported 'improvement'.

Grainger had not always been a poet. He served as a doctor in the army for a time, settling in London upon leaving the armed forces. It was here that he first came into contact with Dr Johnson's circle. Grainger began to write and publish. His principal work was entitled 'An Obstinate Case of Dysentery Cured by Limewater'. Grainger went to Jamaica and made money from sugar plantations, returning to London to publish his poem on the subject. He died of fever in Jamaica in 1767.

The first extract below concerns the fraudulent designs of the French, who 'Mix with their sugar loads of worthless sand, / Fraudful, their weight of sugar to increase'. Such artfulness is beyond the capability of Britain's dim-witted sugar salesmen. The second extract tells of the 'bugs of uncommon shape' that plague the planters. The choosing of slaves is addressed in the third extract, where the reader is exhorted to ensure that his would-be slaves have red tongues and flat stomachs, and the ailments of slaves are considered in the fourth. The fifth extract reveals that the Muse does not disdain to sing of compost. The reader is given some useful advice: 'Never, ah! never, be asham'd to tread / Thy dung heaps'.

*From* **The Sugar Cane**

From Book I

False Gallia's sons, that hoe the ocean isles,
Mix with their sugar loads of worthless sand,
Fraudful, their weight of sugar to increase.
Far be such guile from Britain's honest swains.
Such arts, awhile, th' unwary may surprise,
And benefit th' imposter; but, ere long,
The skilful buyer will the fraud detect,
And, with abhorrence, reprobate the name.

# The World's Worst Poetry

From Book II

And pity the poor planter, when the blast,
Fell plague of Heaven! perdition of the isles!
Attacks his waving gold. Though well-manur'd;
A richness through thy fields from Nature boast;
Though seasons pour; this pestilence invades:
Too oft it seizes the glad infant throng,
Nor pities their green nonage: their broad blades,
Of which the graceful wood-nymphs erst compos'd
The greenest garlands to adorn their brows,
First pallid, sickly, dry, and wither'd show;
Unseemly stains succeed; which, nearer view'd
By microscopic arts, small eggs appear,
Dire fraught with reptile life; alas, too soon
They burst their filmy gaol, and crawl abroad,
Bugs of uncommon shape...

From Book III

Must thou from Afric reinforce thy gang?
Let health and youth their every sinew firm;
Clear roll their ample eye; their tongue be red;
Broad swell their chest; their shoulders wide expand;
Not prominent their belly; clean and strong
Their thighs and legs, in just proportion rise.
Such soon will brave the fervours of the clime;

And free from ails, that kill thy Negro-train,
An useful servitude will long support.

From Book IV

One precept more, it much imports to know.
The Blacks, who drink the Quanza's lucid stream,
Fed by ten thousand streams, are prone to bloat,
Whether at home or in these ocean isles:
And though nice art the water may subdue,
Yet many die; and few, for many a year,
Just strength attain to labour their lord.
Wouldst thou secure thine Ethiop from these ails,
Which change of climate, change of waters breed,
And food unusual? let Machaon draw
From each some blood, as age and sex require.

From Book V

Of composts shall the Muse distain to sing?
Nor soil her heavenly plumes? The sacred Muse
Nought sordid deems, but what is base; nought fair,
Unless true Virtue stamp it with her seal.
Then, planter, wouldst thou double thine estate,
Never, ah! never, be asham'd to tread
Thy dung heaps...

## John, Lord HERVEY
## (1696–1743)

Lord Hervey was a moderately successful politician and a terrible poet. He supported Pulteney on the opposition benches, but deserted to serve under Walpole, whom George II had appointed as Prime Minister. Walpole himself never liked Hervey, saying in 1742, a year before Hervey's death, that Hervey was 'as full of his dirty little politics as ever'.

The politician George Canning later parodied Hervey's verse: 'The feathered tribes on pinions swim the air; / Not so the Mackerel, and still less the Bear'. The original poems are so bizarre as to be beyond parody. The image of a mole exploring a lake in a fit of 'wanton madness' is a high point in absurdity. The brief discursion on the sexual desires of birds and fish is equally delightful. It has been called 'as reasoned a plea for farmyard morals as any advanced thinker of today could desire'.

*From* **Epistle to Mr Fox, from Hampton Court**

From Book I

Will the wise Elephant desert the wood,
To imitate the whale and range the flood?

Or will the Mole her native earth forsake,
In wanton madness to explore the lake?

From Book II

Would any feather'd maiden of the wood,
Or scaly female of the peopled flood,
When lust and hunger call'd, its force resist?
In abstinence or charity persist?
And cry, "If Heaven's intent were understood,
These tastes were only given to be withstood"?
Or would they wisely both these gifts improve,
And eat when hungry, and when am'rous love?

# William IGGLESDEN
## (fl. 1858)

William Igglesden, a Commander in Her Majesty's
Indian Navy, wrote poetical miscellanies. In 1858 a
collection of his verse was published under the
somewhat predictable title *Poetical Miscellanea by A
Commander of Her Majesty's Indian Navy*. The
collection is unusual for many reasons, not least because
it contains a poem addressed to an iceberg. The iceberg
in question is quizzed on its provenance and future
travelling arrangements.

## To an Iceberg in the Southern Ocean

Antarctic wanderer, whither art thou roaming?
And what is thy past history?
Who, on the boisterous surge, amid night's gloaming,
Seemest to us a mystery.

At dawn of day, or at meridian tide,
Or when Sol'd orb at eve refulgent shines;
Beauty iridescent illumes thy side,
Like unto dazzling crystal mines.

Which nature's bounty, oft with lavish hand,
Profusely spreads beneath in proud display;
Enshrined in distant, as in Britain's land,
Obscured from garish light of day.

Yet to the mariner, when tempest tost,
Thy presence brings to him but sore dismay;
Contact with thee, all hope were surely lost,
Death then engulfs his helpless prey.

# Edward JOHNSON
## (fl. 1880s)

The next poem is awarded a place in this book on account of the poet's maniacal and alarming devotion to water, which borders, perhaps, on the fanatical. 'Oh! water for me! Bright water for me!' says Johnson. Wine, it seems, is good enough only for the tremulous debauchee. Water, on the other hand, has a variety of unsubstantiated and unsustainable claims made for it. He claims, amongst other things, that it strengthens the limbs and extends the life of pensioners. Certainly the aforementioned pensioners would not survive for long if they were deprived of water altogether, but one suspects that they would be happier with the wine so irresponsibly lavished on the debauchee. Johnson, it seems, is too devoted to water to consider the alternatives. 'Hurrah! for bright water! hurrah, hurrah!'

### The Water-Drinker

Oh! water for me! Bright water for me!
And wine for the tremulous debauchee!
It cooleth the brow, it cooleth the brain,
It maketh the faint one strong again;
It comes o'er the sense like a breeze from the sea,
All freshness, like infant purity.

Oh! water, bright water for me, for me!
Give wine, give wine to the debauchee!

Fill to the brim! Fill, fill to the brim!
Let the flowing crystal kiss the rim!
For my hand is steady, my eye is true,
For I, like the flowers, drink nought but dew.
Oh! water, bright water's a mine of wealth,
And the ores it yieldeth are vigour and health.
So water, pure water, for me, for me!
And wine for the tremulous debauchee!

Fill again to the brim! again to the brim!
For water strengtheneth life and limb!
To the days of the aged it addeth length,
To the might of the strong it addeth strength.
It freshens the heart, it brightens the sight,
'Tis like quaffing a goblet of morning light!
So, Water! I will drink nought but thee,
Thou parent of health and energy!

When o'er the hills, like a gladsome bride,
Morning walks forth in her beauty's pride,
And, leading a band of laughing hours,
Brushes the dew from the nodding flowers;
Oh! cheerily then my voice is heard,
Mingling with that of the soaring bird,

Who flingeth abroad his matins loud,
As he freshens his wings in the cold grey cloud.

But when Evening has quitted her sheltering yew,
Drowsily flying and weaving anew
Her dusky meshes o'er land and sea —
How gently, O sleep! fall thy poppies on me;
For I drink water, pure, cold, and bright,
And my dreams are of heaven the livelong night;
So, hurrah! for thee, Water! hurrah, hurrah!
Thou art silver and gold, thou art riband and star!
Hurrah! for bright water! hurrah, hurrah!

## Theophilus MARZIALS
## (fl. 1873)

The minor Pre-Raphaelite poet Theophilus Marzials has
been largely forgotten. 'The editors of anthologies of the
literature of the Victorian period ignore Marzials
completely,' wrote a fretful scholar from the University of
Beirut in 1974. That Marzials has been ignored is not
surprising. He received little acclaim during his lifetime.
He worked at British Museum as a Junior Assistant in
the Principal Librarian's Office, an amiable oddball who
dabbled in verse. Marzials' contemporary William Bell
Scott regarded him as 'a noble eccentric man'.

# The World's Worst Poetry

He made the acquaintance of Dante Gabriel Rossetti, to whom he sent an advance copy of his first volume of verse. Rossetti replied in a letter to Marzials dated 20 April 1873. 'I think you have made an unfortunate choice for your leading poem,' wrote Rossetti. 'The Gallery of Pigeons, besides the objection of its odd title, labours more under a throng of puerile perversities in diction than any piece in the volume.' Nevertheless, *The Gallery of Pigeons and Other Poems* was published in 1873, Marzials' first and only book.

The leading Marzials scholar, Professor John Munro, describes Marzials' writing as 'repetitive,' adding that 'his mannered artificiality can be exasperating'. Yet, according to Munro, Marzials at his best displayed 'a remarkable inventive fancy and considerable metrical virtuosity'. Munro concludes by saying that Marzials 'could on occasion produce verses of enduring quality'. I advise you not to rely too heavily on Munro's judgment. The following verses certainly have an enduring quality, but I am not sure what that quality is. Judge for yourself.

*From* The Sun of my Songs

O my heart, and O my head!
Go a-singing a silly song,
    All wrong,
        For all is dead,
            Ding, dong,

And I am dead,
                    Dong!

## A Tragedy
            Death!
            Plop.
The barges down in the river flop.
                    Flop, plop.
            Above, beneath.
From the slimy branches the grey drips drop,
As they scraggle black on the thin grey sky,
Where the black cloud rack-hackles drizzle and fly
To the oozy waters, that lounge and flop
On the black scrag piles, where the loose cords plop,
As the raw wind whines in the thin tree-top.
                    Plop, plop.
            And scudding by
The boatmen call out hoy! and hey!
All is running water and sky,
            And my head shrieks — 'Stop,'
            And my heart shrieks — 'Die.'

My thought is running out of my head;
My love is running out of my heart,
My soul runs after, and leaves me as dead,
For my life runs after to catch them — and fled
They all are every one! — and I stand, and start,

At the water that oozes up, plop and plop,
On the barges that flop
       And dizzy me dead.
       I might reel and drop.
           Plop.
           Dead.
And the shrill wind whines in the thin tree-top
       Flop, plop.


A curse on him.
             Ugh! yet I knew – I knew –
If a woman is false can a friend be true?
It was only a lie from beginning to end –
       My Devil – My 'Friend'
I had trusted the whole of my living to!
       Ugh; and I knew!
           Ugh!
       So what do I care,
And my head is empty as air –
           I can do,
           I can dare,
     (Plop, plop
     The barges flop
     Drip, drop.)
           I can dare, I can dare!
And let myself all run away with my head
And stop.
       Drop

Dead.

        Plop, flop.

        Plop.


# William McGONAGALL
# (1830–1902)

William Topaz McGonagall has a good claim to be inferior to every other versifier in the history of poetry. 'Few people have acquired a niche in history by producing what nobody wanted in a manner nobody applauded,' wrote one critic. Indeed, McGonagall has been called 'The World's Worst Poet' more frequently than I care to remember. Dundee City Council has named him 'The World's Best Bad Poet'.

He was called many other things during his life, most of which, it must be admitted, were abusive. His public verse readings were noted for the appearance of vocal hecklers. When he performed in public houses, waiters threw wet towels at him and publicans threw peas. In his naivety, McGonagall assumed that they objected to the teetotal tone of his poems rather than to the abysmal standard of his verse.

McGonagall was born to poor Irish parents in Edinburgh in 1825. The family moved to Dundee while he was still a boy. His father was a handloom weaver, and McGonagall followed him into this trade. McGonagall married Miss Jean King in 1846. Some years later he began to participate in amateur dramatics, acting in Shakespeare's plays at the Dundee theatre. Through Shakespeare McGonagall found poetry. 'The most startling incident in my life,' he wrote, 'was the time I discovered myself to be a poet.' He continued:

'I seemed to feel as it were a strange kind of feeling stealing over me, and remained so for about five minutes. A flame, as Lord Byron has said, seemed to kindle up my entire frame, along with a strong desire to write poetry; and I felt so happy, so happy, that I was inclined to dance.'

As Derek Wilson has written: 'Throughout the remaining 24 years of McGonagall's life he poured forth a torrent of bad verse, devoid of all metre and scansion, never dignified by any flash of poetic insight, seldom rising above the utterly banal.' It has been written that by another critic that 'he had no ear for metre, a knack for choosing the most banal of subjects, and a tendency to stretch mightily for a rhyme'. The poverty of his verses was in stark contrast to the magnificent subjects about which he chose to write. It is notable that he was moved predominantly by grand spectacles, horrific catastrophes, and unusual events.

His first collection, *Poetic Gems*, was published in 1878. In his lifetime, he published volumes, entitled, in order of their appearance, *More Poetic Gems, Still More Poetic Gems, Yet More Poetic Gems, Further Poetic Gems, Yet Further Poetic Gems* and *Last Poetic Gems*. As his fame grew, he toured Scotland, England, and the United States, giving public readings for which he charged admission and at which he dressed in full Scottish Highland costume. He is reported to have been a cult figure in his lifetime, although his audiences were often rather turbulent.

The notion of a terrible and talentless poet trapped by naïve Romanticism appealed to the comedian Spike Milligan, who appeared as McGonagall in the film *The Great McGonagall*, which starred Peter Sellers as Queen Victoria. In the same year, a bad poetry competition was organised in which poets of McGonagall's calibre were sought. Cash prizes were offered. Peter Sellers and Spike Milligan were among the panel of judges. No winner was declared. All entries were rejected. The judges declared that no poet could yet compare with William McGonagall. This is as true now, I think, as it was then. The poetry of McGonagall is still in print today. It has been translated into Russian, Japanese, Thai, Bulgarian, Romanian and Chinese. Never has a failure been so successful.

## Attempted Assassination of the Queen

God prosper long our noble Queen,
And long may she reign!
Maclean he tried to shoot her,
But it was all in vain.

For God He turned the ball aside
Maclean aimed at her head;
And he felt very angry
Because he didn't shoot her dead.

There's a divinity that hedges a king,
And so it does seem,
And my opinion is, it has hedged
Our most gracious Queen.

Maclean must be a madman,
Which is obvious to be seen,
Or else he wouldn't have tried to shoot
Our most beloved Queen.

Victoria is a good Queen,
Which all her subjects know,
And for that God has protected her
From all her deadly foes.

She is noble and generous,
Her subjects must confess;
There hasn't been her equal
Since the days of good Queen Bess.

Long may she be spared to roam
Among the bonnie Highland floral,
And spend many a happy day
In the palace of Balmoral.

Because she is very kind
To the old women there,
And allows them bread, tea, and sugar,
And each one get a share.

And when they know of her coming,
Their hearts feel overjoy'd,
Because, in general, she finds work
For men that's unemploy'd.

And she also gives the gipsies money
While at Balmoral, I've been told,
And, mind ye, seldom silver,
But very often gold.

I hope God will protect her
By night and by day,

At home and abroad,
When she's far away.

May He be as a hedge around her,
As he's been all along,
And let her live and die in peace
Is the end of my song.

## The Sorrows of the Blind

Pity the sorrows of the poor blind,
For they can but little comfort find;
As they walk along the street,
They know not where to put their feet.
They are deprived of that earthly joy
Of seeing either man, woman, or boy;
Sad and lonely through the world they go,
Not knowing a friend from a foe:
Nor the difference betwixt day and night,
For the want of their eyesight;
The blind mother cannot see her darling boy,
That was once her soul's joy.
By day and night,
Since she lost her precious sight;
To her the world seems dark and drear,
And she can find no comfort here.
She once found pleasure in reading books,

But now pale and careworn are her looks.
Since she has lost her eyesight,
Everything seems wrong and nothing right.

The face of nature, with all its beauties and livery
green,
Appears to the blind just like a dream.
All things beautiful have vanished from their sight,
Which were once their heart's delight.
The blind father cannot see his beautiful child, nor
wife,
That was once the joy of his life;
That he was wont to see at morn and night,
When he had his eyesight.
All comfort has vanished from him now,
And a dejected look hangs on his brow.

Kind Christians all, both great and small,
Pity the sorrows of the blind,
They can but little comfort find;
Therefore we ought to be content with our lot,
And for the eyesight we have got,
And pray to God both day and night
To preserve our eyesight;
To be always willing to help the blind in their distress,
And the Lord will surely bless
And guard us by night and day,
And remember us at the judgment day.

## An Address to the Rev. George Gilfillan

All hail to the Rev. George Gilfillan of Dundee,
He is the greatest preacher I did ever hear or see.
He is a man of genius bright,
And in him his congregation does delight,
Because they find him to be honest and plain,
Affable in temper, and seldom known to complain.
He preaches in a plain straightforward way,
The people flock to hear him night and day,
And hundreds from the doors are often turn'd away,
Because he is the greatest preacher of the present day.
He has written the life of Sir Walter Scott,
And while he lives he will never be forgot,
Nor when he is dead.
Because by his admirers it will be often read;
And fill their minds with wonder and delight,
And while away the tedious hours on a cold winter's
night.
He has also written about the Bards of the Bible,
Which occupied nearly three years in which he was
not idle,
Because when he sits down to write he does it with
might and main,
And to get an interview with him it would be almost
vain,
And in that he is always right,

For the Bible tells us whatever your hands findeth to
                                                    do,
Do it with all your might.
Rev. George Gilfillan of Dundee, I must conclude my
                                                  muse,
And to write in praise of thee my pen does not refuse,
Nor does it give me pain to tell the world fearlessly,
                                              that when
You are dead they shall not look upon your like again.

## The Albion Battleship Calamity

'Twas in the year of 1898, and on the 21st of June,
The launching of the Battleship Albion caused a great
                                                  gloom,
Amongst the relatives of many persons who were
                            drowned in the River Thames,
Which their relatives will remember while life
                                               remains.

The vessel was christened by the Duchess of York,
And the spectators' hearts felt as light as cork
As the Duchess cut the cord that was holding the fine
                                                  ship,
Then the spectators loudly cheered as the vessel slid
                                          down the slip.

The launching of the vessel was very well carried out,
While the guests on the stands cheered without any
doubt,
Under the impression that everything would go well;
But, alas! instantaneously a bridge and staging fell.

Oh! little did the Duchess of York think that day
That so man lives would be taken away
At the launching of the good ship Albion,
But when she heard of the catastrophe she felt woebe
gone.

But accidents will happen without any doubt,
And often the cause thereof is hard to find out;
And according to report, I've heard people say,
'Twas the great crowd on the bridge caused it to give
way.

Just as the vessel entered the water the bridge and
staging gave way,
Immersing three hundred people which caused great
dismay
Amongst thousands of spectators that were standing
there,
And in the faces of the bystanders were depicted
despair.

Then the police boats instantly made for the fatal
spot,
And with the aid of dockyard hands several people
were got,
While some scrambled out themselves, the best they
could —
And the most of them were inhabitants of the
neighbourhood.

Part of them were the wives and daughters of the
dockyard hands,
And as they gazed upon them they in amazement
stands;
And several bodies were hauled up quite dead.
Which filled the onlookers' hearts with pity and
dread.

One of the first rescued was a little baby,
Which was conveyed away to a mortuary;
And several were taken to the fitter's shed, and
attended to there
By the fireman and several nurses with the greatest care.

Meanwhile heartrending scenes were taking place,
Whilst the tears ran down many a Mother and
Father's face,
That had lost their children in the River Thames,

Which they will remember while life remains.

Oh, Heaven! it was horrible to see the bodies laid out
                          in rows,
As Fathers and Mothers passed along, adown their
                          cheeks the tears flows,
While their poor, sickly hearts were throbbing with
                          fear.
A great crowd had gathered to search for the missing
                          dead,
And many strong men broke down because their heart
                          pity bled,
As they looked upon the distorted faces of their
                          relatives dear,
While adown their cheeks flowed many a silent tear.

The tenderest sympathy, no doubt, was shown to
                          them,
By the kind hearted Police and Firemen;
The scene in fact was most sickening to behold,
And enough to make one's blood run cold,
To see tear-stained men and women there
Searching for their relatives, and in their eyes a pitiful
                          stare.

There's one brave man in particular I must mention,
And I'm sure he's worthy of the people's attention.

His name is Thomas Cooke, of No. 6 Percy Road,
                                    Canning Town,
Whose name ought to be to posterity handed down,
Because he leapt into the River Thames, and hero-
                                    ically did behave,
And rescued five persons from a watery grave.

Mr Wilson, a young Electrician, got a terrible fright,
When he saw his mother and sister dead — he was
                                    shocked at the sight,
Because his sister had not many days returned from
                                    her honeymoon,
And in his countenance, alas! there was a sad gloom.

Her Majesty has sent a message of sympathy to the
                                    bereaved ones in distress,
And the Duke and Duchess of York have sent 25
                                    guineas I must confess,
And £1,000 from the Directors of the Thames
                                    Ironworks and Shipbuilding Company,
Which I hope will help to fill the bereaved ones'
                                    hearts with glee.

And in conclusion I will venture to say,
That accidents will happen by night and by day;
And I will say without any fear,
Because to me it appears quite clear,

That the stronger we our houses do build,
The less chance we have of being killed.

# James McINTYRE
# (1827–1906)

James McIntyre has been honoured posthumously with
the title 'Canada's Worst Poet'. It is an honour he
deserves. McIntyre was born in Forres, Scotland and
emigrated to Canada in 1841 at the age of 14. First he
worked as an agricultural labourer, clearing land and
collecting maple sap. He then became a furniture dealer
in Ontario, eventually establishing a furniture factory in
Ingersoll, Ontario. This small town of little over five
thousand inhabitants was in Oxford County, the heart of
Canada's dairy industry.

It was here that McIntyre heard the call of the Muse.
He published two volumes of his collected poems. The
first, entitled *Musings on the Banks of Canadian Thames*, was
published in 1884. The second, *The Poems of James
McIntyre*, saw the light of day in 1889. McIntyre's poems
covered a large number of different themes, including
but not limited to Canadian literature, the towns of
Ontario, agriculture, patriotism, and poets and philoso-

phers. McIntyre is most famous for his verses on the theme of cheese. It was here that wrote his best works. 'There is nothing insignificant about McIntyre's poetry,' writes one commentator, 'for it is a landmark in dairy-based literature.'

'We received so many kind assurances from friends in this neighbourhood and from gentlemen at a distance who had taken an interest in our first little work,' wrote McIntyre in the introduction to his second book, 'that they induce us to issue this more comprehensive volume containing about one hundred new pieces. We have written a number of dairy odes recently; these and our patriotic songs composed during the last year we trust will make the work more interesting. We publish a few short pieces from the many letters and poems we received from friends. We hope the public will peruse the poems in a friendly spirit.'

He explained his 'Dairy and Cheese Odes' as follows: 'As cheese making first began in this county and it has already become the chief industry of many counties, it is no insignificant theme. About the middle of this century Canada was a great importer of cheese, and now cheese is the principal article of export from the Province of Ontario, and this Province will soon export no less than ten million dollars worth of cheese per annum.'

The introduction was followed by 'Short Extracts

from Letters Received by the Author' praising the first book. McIntyre reported that the following lines were received from Mr William Murray of Hamilton:

> In writing you do not pretend
> With Tennysonian themes to blend.
> It is an independent style
> Begotten on Canadian soil.

'The Editor of the Toronto Globe,' claimed McIntyre, 'after reviewing a number other books pronounced our little volume to be the gem of the table.' McIntyre continued:

'Colonel Denison, Toronto's police magistrate, "found many interesting pieces on Canadian subjects in the volume." Joaquin Miller, the American poet, hailed me as "my dear poet of the Canadian pasture fields," and he said I did wisely in singing of useful themes. Dr Scadding, the Antiquarian, thought my poem on Father Ranney, the cheese pioneer, "had the ring of a fine old ballad about it." The Honourable Oliver Mowat was pleased with the patriotic spirit displayed in the poems.'

The 'Ode on the Mammoth Cheese,' the 'Oxford Cheese Ode' and 'Prophecy of a Ten Ton Cheese' are the best of McIntyre's cheese poems. The poem on Father Ranney, the Cheese Pioneer, is included so that the reader may decide whether or not it can be said to have

the ring of a fine old ballad about it. McIntyre's short
poem on Shelley is a masterpiece.

## Ode on the Mammoth Cheese, Weight Over Seven Thousand Pounds

We have seen thee, queen of cheese,
Lying quietly at your ease,
Gently fanned by evening breeze,
Thy fair form no flies dare seize.

All gaily dressed soon you'll go
To the great Provincial show,
To be admired by many a beau
In the city of Toronto.

Cows numerous as a swarm of bees,
Or as the leaves upon the trees,
It did require to make thee please,
And stand unrivalled, queen of cheese.

May you not receive a scar as
We have heard that Mr. Harris
Intends to send you off as far as
The great world's show at Paris.

Of the youth beware of these,
For some of them might rudely squeeze

And bite your cheek, then songs or glees
We could not sing, oh! queen of cheese.

We'rt thou suspended from balloon,
You'd cast a shade even at noon,
Folks would think it was the moon
About to fall and crush them soon.

## Oxford Cheese Ode

The ancient poets ne'er did dream
That Canada was land of cream,
They ne'er imagined it could flow
In this cold land of ice and snow,
Where everything did solid freeze,
They ne'er hoped or looked for cheese.

A few years since our Oxford farms
Were nearly robbed of all their charms,
O'er cropped the weary land grew poor
And nearly barren as a moor,
But now the owners live at ease
Rejoicing in their crop of cheese.

And since they justly treat the soil,
Are well rewarded for their toil,
The land enriched by goodly cows,

Yields plenty now to fill their mows,
Both wheat and barley, oats and peas
But still their greatest boast is cheese.

And you must careful fill your mows
With good provender for your cows,
And in the winter keep them warm,
Protect them safe all time from harm,
For cows do dearly love their ease,
Which doth insure best grade of cheese.

To us it is a glorious theme
To sing of milk and curds and cream,
Were it collected it could float
On its bosom, small steam boat,
Cows numerous as swarm of bees
Are milked in Oxford to make cheese.

## Prophecy of a Ten Ton Cheese

In presenting this delicate, dainty morsel to the
imagination of the people, I believed that it could be
realized. I viewed the machine that turned and raised the
mammoth cheese, and saw the powerful machine
invented by James Ireland at the West Oxford
companies factory to turn the great and fine cheese he was
making there. This company with but little
assistance could produce a ten ton cheese.

Who hath prophetic vision sees
In future times a ten ton cheese,
Several companies could join
To furnish curd for great combine
More honour far than making gun
Of mighty size and many a ton.
Machine it could be made with ease
That could turn this monster cheese,
The greatest honour to our land
Would be this orb of finest brand,
Three hundred curd they would need squeeze
For to make this mammoth cheese.
So British lands could confederate
Three hundred provinces in one state,
When all in harmony agrees
To be pressed in one like this cheese,
Then one skilful hand could acquire
Power to move British empire.
But various curds must be combined
And each factory their curd must grind,
To blend harmonious in one
This great cheese of mighty span,
And uniform in quality
A glorious reality.
But it will need a powerful press
This cheese queen to caress,
And a large extent of charms

Hoop will encircle in its arms,
And we do not now despair,
But we shall see it at world's fair.
And view the people all agog, so
Excited o'er it in Chicago,
To seek fresh conquests queen of cheese
She may sail across the seas,
Where she would meet reception grand
From the warm hearts in old England.

## Father Ranney, the Cheese Pioneer

When Father Ranney left the States,
In Canada to try the fates,
He settled down in Dereham,
Then no dairyman lived near him;
He was the first there to squeeze
His cow's milk into good cheese,
And at each Provincial show
His famed cheese was all the go.
Then long life to Father Ranney
May he wealth and honour gain aye.
He always took the first prize
Both for quality and size,
But many of his neighbours
Now profit by his labours,
And the ladies dress in silk

From the proceeds of the milk,
But those who buy their butter,
How dear it is, they mutter.
Then long life to Father Ranney
May he wealth and honour gain aye.
Now we close this glorious theme,
This song of curds and rich cream,
You can buy your hoops and screws,
And all supplies for dairy use,
Milk cans and vats, all things like these
In Ingersoll great mart for cheese,
Here buyers do congregate
And pay for cheese the highest rate.
So we call on you again aye,
To honour Father Ranney.

### Shelley

We have scarcely time to tell thee
Of the strange and gifted Shelley,
Kind hearted man but ill-fated,
So youthful, drowned and cremated.

# James MILLIGAN
## (fl. 1800s)

The reader need know no more about James Milligan
than that he was fascinated by geology. The extract below
is taken from his masterpiece, the poem 'Geology', in
which the subject was stretched to some 600 lines. The
reader, it is hoped, will be filled with 'thoughts profound'
whilst contemplating the implications of fossils.

### *From* Geology

The science of Geology
Proves the earth's great antiquity.
We find, when we look well abroad,
The rocks contain their own record.
Each age of the world they make known;
Each series of rocks has its own.
The animal and plant remains
Conclusive evidence sustains
They lived on the earth's surface fair
When the huge rocks were forming there.
Sunlight and air, water and land,
Sustained them 'mid fair Nature grand.
In ages past they lived and died,
And afterwards were petrified
By enclosure in massive rocks,

And thus became fossilised blocks.
The oldest-known rocks contain lime,
Thus proving at that remote time
Animal life did then abound,
Which may fill us with thought profound.


## Harry Edward MILLS
(fl. 1870s)

Little need be said about the sheer brilliance of the poem
below. Rarely have the words 'vociferate' and 'vocalise'
been used to describe frogs. Never, to my knowledge, has
their 'monotone uncouth' been so celebrated in verse.

### The Early Frogs

O, I love to hear the frogs
When they first begin to sing;
How they vocalise the bogs,
And vociferate the Spring.
How they carol as they croak,
How they mingle jest and joke
With their solemn chant and dirge
On the river's slimy verge.

O, I love to hear the frogs,
For their monotone uncouth
Is the music of the cogs
Of the mill wheel of my youth.
And I listen half asleep,
And the eyes of mem'ry peep
Through the bars that hold me fast,
From the pleasures of the past.

O, I love to hear the frogs,
For their melody is health
To the heart that worry flogs
With the lash of want or wealth.
And the cares of life take wing,
And its pleasures lose their sting,
And love's channel way unclogs
In the croaking of the frogs.

## Julia A. MOORE
## (1847–1920)

It is no exaggeration to say that Julia A. Moore wrote
some of the worst poetry ever to have been published in
the United States of America. 'Shakespeare, could he
read it, would be glad that he was dead,' wrote a

contemporary critic. 'If Julia A. Moore would kindly deign to shed some of her poetry on our humble grave, we should be but too glad to go out and shoot ourselves tomorrow.' The publisher, J. F. Ryder, of Cleveland, Ohio, had anticipated otherwise, thinking that the poems would 'divert the despondent from suicide'.

Bereavement was a theme to which Mrs Moore returned with a frequency as alarming as it was predictable. Most common were poems about the tragic and untimely deaths of local children. Mrs Moore would dash off an elegy before the body was cold. 'Little Henry', reprinted below, is a classic of its kind. One critic thought that 'to meet such steady and unremitting demands on the tear ducts a person should instead be equipped with a water main'.

Her first volume of verse, entitled *The Sweet Singer of Michigan Salutes the Public*, was published in 1876. Mrs Moore ranged over numerous subjects, gleaning her inspiration from newspaper stories and rural gossip as well as from the deaths of neighbours and their children. Her poems were not intended to be amusing, but laughter was the most common reaction to her verse. Mark Twain loved it and said that it was one of the funniest books he had ever read. Later dubbed *The Sentimental Song Book*, it became one of the poetic best sellers of the era.

When browsing through a book of Mrs Moore's poetry, even the most inattentive of readers will realise that something is amiss. She has a heady disregard for grammar and a reckless enthusiasm for forcing unsuitable words to rhyme. She has, as Mark Twain noted, an uncanny ability to make an intentionally humorous episode pathetic and an intentionally pathetic one funny. The inept simplicity of sentiment is one of the more obvious of her literary misdeeds. The unrelenting artlessness, the naïveté and the bewildered optimism mark out her poetry as truly and wonderfully abysmal.

## The Author's Early Life

I will write a sketch of my early life,
It will be of childhood day,
And all who chance to read it,
No criticism, pray.
My childhood days were happy,
And it fills my heart with woe,
To muse o'er the days that have passed by
And the scenes of long ago.
In the days of my early childhood,
Kent county was quite wild,
Especially the towns I lived in
When I was a little child.
I will not speak of my birthplace,
For if you will only look
O'er the little poem, 'My Childhood Days,'
That is in this little book.

I am not ashamed of my birthright,
Though it was of poor estate,
Many a poor person in our land
Has risen to be great.
My parents were poor, I know, kind friends,
But that is no disgrace;
They were honourable and respected
Throughout my native place.

My mother was an invalid,
And was for many a year,
And I being the eldest daughter
Her life I had to cheer.
I had two little sisters,
And a brother which made three,
And dear mother being sickly,
Their care it fell on me.

My parents moved to Algoma
Near twenty-three years ago,
And bought one hundred acres of land,
That's a good sized farm you know.
It was then a wilderness,
With tall forest trees abound,
And it was four miles from a village,
Or any other town.

And it was two miles from a schoolhouse,
That's the distance I had to go,
And how many times I travelled
Through summer suns and winter snow.
How well do I remember
Going to school many a morn,
Both in summer and in winter,
Through many a heavy storm.

My heart was gay and happy,
This was ever in my mind,
There is better times a coming,
And I hope some day to find
Myself capable of composing.
It was by heart's delight,
To compose on a sentimental subject
If it came in my mind just right.

If I went to school half the time,
It was all that I could do;
It seems very strange to me sometimes,
And it may seem strange to you.
It was natural for me to compose,
And put words into rhyme,
And the success of my first work
Is this little song book of mine.

My childhood days have passed and gone,
And it fills my heart with pain
To think that youth will nevermore
Return to me again.
And now kind friends, what I have wrote,
I hope you will pass o'er,
And not criticise as some have done,
Hitherto herebefore.

## Temperance Reform Clubs

Some enterprising people,
In our cities and towns,
Have gone to organizing clubs
Of men that's fallen down;
In estimation fallen low —
Now they may rise again,
And be respected citizens
Throughout our native land.

The temperance reform club,
Forever may it stand,
And everyone that loves strong drink
Pray, join it heart and hand.
Then many a home will be bright,
And many a heart made glad,
It will be the greatest blessing
This nation ever had.

Manufacturers of strong drink
Can find better employ,
Than bring to ruin poor families,
And thousand souls destroy,
Likewise proprietors of saloons
Lose many a customer;
Those men now rather stay at home,
That place they now prefer.

Don't be ashamed to wear your badge
Of ribbon on your breast,
It shows you've joined the club to be
A man among the rest.
Your kindred friends will love to see
You honoured, sober man,
And all the friends that wish you well
Will help you if they can.

Perhaps you have a mother,
Likewise a sister, too;
Perhaps you have a sweetheart
That thinks the most of you.
Perhaps you have a loving wife,
And little ones at home,
Their hearts rejoice to see that you
Can let strong drink alone.

Many a man joined the club
That never drank a dram,
Those noble men were kind and brave
They care not for the slang –
The slang they meet on every side:
"You're a reform drunkard, too;
You've joined the red ribbon brigade,
Among the drunkard crew."

It shows their hearts were very kind,
They wish to save poor souls
That loved the intoxication cup,
That signed the temperance roll.
Dear friends, ever keep rolling
The work you have begun,
Those noble men will not repent,
I hope, throughout our land.

Dr. Reynolds is a noble man,
He has worked hard to save
Some people in our cities and towns,
From out a drunkard's grave.
There is other men to help him now,
He lectures not alone
Many a heart that blesses them
From out now happy homes.

## Grand Rapids Cricket Club

In Grand Rapids is a handsome club,
Of men that cricket play,
As fine a set of skillful men
That can their skill display.
They are the champions of the West,
They think they are quite fine,
They've won a hundred honours well;
It is their most cunning design.

Brave Kelso, he's considered great,
Chief of the club he is found;
Great crowds he draws to see him bowl
The ball upon the ground.
And Mr. Follet is very brave,
A lighter player than the rest,
He got struck severe at the fair ground
For which he took a rest.

When Mr Dennis does well play,
His courage is full great,
And accidents to him occur,
But not much, though, of late.
This ball play is a dangerous game,
Brave knights to play it though;
Those boys would be the nation's pride,
If they to war would go.

From Milwaukee their club did come,
With thoughts of skill at play,
But beat they was, and then went home —
Had nothing more to say.
Grand Rapids club that cricket play,
Will soon be known afar,
Much prouder do the members stand,
Like many a noble star.

## Little Henry

Oh! come listen to my story
Of a little infant child —
His spirit is in glory —
It has left us for a while.
Death has robbed us of our Henry,
He is with our Saviour now,
Where there is no pain or sorrow
Comes to cloud his little brow.

God has took their little treasure,
And his name I'll tell you now,
He has gone from earth forever,
Their little Charles Henry House.

His cheeks were red as roses,
And his eyes were black as coals,

His little lips were red as rubies,
And his little hair it curled.
Oh, they called him little Charley,
He was full of joyful mirth —
Now his little form is lying
'Neath the cold and silent earth.

It was the eleventh of December,
On a cold and windy day,
Just at the close of evening,
When the sunlight fades away;
Little Henry he was dying,
In his little crib he lay,
With soft winds round him sighing
From the morn till close of day.

Parents, brothers, sisters weeping,
For their cup of sorrow's full,
And his little playthings keeping,
That he thought so beautiful —
Tears from parents' eyes were starting
For their little loving one.
Oh! how painful was the parting
From their little infant son.

Oh! how often have they kissed him,
And caressed his little brow —
To his little voice have listened,

But his place is vacant now.
They called him little Charley,
And his loving name they called,
But they could not keep their darling
From the loving Saviour's call.

But they must now cease their mourning,
His little soul is at rest,
Where there can no storms of trouble
Roll across his peaceful breast.
Now his little form is sleeping
In the cold and silent tomb,
And his friends are left a weeping,
In his dear and loving home.

It was the eleventh of December,
Eighteen seventy was the year,
Kind friends will all remember –
Silently let fall a tear.
But we must not trouble borrow,
For the God of heaven is just;
No one knows a parent's sorrow,
Till a child some friend have lost.

## Ashtabula Disaster

Have you heard of the dreadful fate
Of Mr. P. P. Bliss and wife?
Of their death I will relate,
And also others lost their life;
In the Ashtabula Bridge disaster,
Where so many people died
Without a thought that destruction
Would plunge them 'neath the wheel of tide.

Among the ruins are many friends,
Crushed to death amidst the roar;
On one thread all may depend,
And hope they've reached the other shore.
P. P. Bliss showed great devotion
To his faithful wife, his pride,
When he saw that she must perish,
He died a martyr by her side.

P. P. Bliss went home above –
Left all friends, earth and fame,
To rest in God's holy love;
Left on earth his work and name.
The people love his work by numbers,
It is read by great and small,
He by it will be remembered,
He has left it for us all.

His good name from time to time
Will rise on land and sea;
It is known in distant climes,
Let it echo wide and free.
One good man among the number,
Found sweet rest in a short time,
His weary soul may sweetly slumber
Within the vale, heaven sublime.

Destruction lay on every side,
Confusion, fire and despair;
No help, no hope, so they died,
Two hundred people over there.
Many ties was there broken,
Many a heart was filled with pain,
Each one left a little token,
For above they live again.

## Lord Byron's Life

"Lord Byron" was an Englishman,
A poet I believe,
His first works in old England
Was poorly received.
Perhaps it was "Lord Byron's" fault
And perhaps it was not.

His life was full of misfortunes,
Ah, strange was his lot.

The character of "Lord Byron"
Was of a low degree,
Caused by his reckless conduct,
And bad company.
He sprung from an ancient house,
Noble, but poor indeed.
His career on earth, was marred
By his own misdeeds.

Generous and tender-hearted,
Affectionate by extreme,
In temper he was wayward,
A poor "Lord" without means;
Ah, he was a handsome fellow
With great poetic skill,
His great intellectual powers
He could use at his will.

He was a sad child of nature,
Of fortune and of fame;
Also sad child to society,
For nothing did he gain
But slander and ridicule,
Throughout his native land.

Thus the "poet of the passions,"
Lived, unappreciated, man.

Yet at the age of twenty-four
"Lord Byron" then had gained
The highest, highest pinnacle
Of literary fame.
Ah, he had such violent passions
They were beyond his control,
Yet the public with its justice
Sometimes would him extol.

Sometimes again "Lord Byron"
Was censured by the press,
Such obloquy, he could not endure,
So he done what was the best.
He left his native country,
This great unhappy man;
The only wish he had, 'tis said,
He might die, sword in hand.

He had joined the Grecian Army;
This man of delicate frame;
And there he died in a distant land,
And left on earth his fame.
"Lord Byron's" age was thirty-six years,
Then closed the sad career,

Of the most celebrated "Englishman"
Of the nineteenth century.

## The Great Chicago Fire

The great Chicago Fire, friends,
Will never be forgot;
In the history of Chicago
It will remain a darken spot.
It was a dreadful horrid sight
To see that City in flames;
But no human aid could save it,
For all skill was tried in vain.

In the year of 1871,
In October on the 8th,
The people in that City, then
Was full of life, and great.
Less than four days it lay in ruins,
That garden City, so great
Lay smouldering in ashes,
In a sad and pitiful state.

It was a sad, sad scene indeed,
To see the fire arise,
And hear the crackling of the flames
As it almost reached the skies,

And sadder still, to hear the moans,
Of people in the flames
Cry for help, and none could get,
Ah, die where they remained.

To see the people run for life;
Up and down the blazing streets,
To find then, their escape cut off
By the fiery flaming sheets,
And others hunting for some friend
That perhaps they never found,
Such weeping, wailing, never was known,
For a thousand miles around.

Some people were very wealthy
On the morning of the 10th.
But at the close of the evening,
Was poor, but felt content,
Glad to escape from harm with life
With friends they loved so well,
Some will try to gain more wisdom,
By the sad sight they beheld.

Five thousand people were homeless,
Sad wanderers in the streets,
With no shelter to cover them,
And no food had they to eat.
They wandered down by the lake side,

Lay down on the cold damp ground,
So tired and weary and homeless,
So the rich, the poor, was found.

Mothers with dear little infants,
Some clinging to the breast.
People of every description
All laid down there to rest,
With the sky as their covering,
Ah, pillows they had none.
Sad, oh sad, it must have been,
For those poor homeless ones.

Neighbouring Cities sent comfort,
To the poor lone helpless ones,
And God will not forget them
In all the years to come.
Now the City of Chicago
Is built up anew once more,
And may it never be visited
With such a great fire no more.

# Edward NEWMAN
## (fl. 1840s)

Edward Newman, the President of the Entomological Society in the mid-nineteenth century, was a prolific writer. His publications included *A Familiar Introduction to the History of Insects*, a reference work containing 'every instruction for catching, killing, classifying, arranging and preserving insects'. We do not know how it was received by his fellow amateur entomologists, but it did have one advantage over its competitors in the entomological book market: as Newman himself liked to point out, it was written in 'the plainest possible phraseology'.

The same is true of his poetic masterpiece, 'The Insect Hunter,' an epic poem some 86 pages in length, which he published in 1855. The poem, which Newman thoughtfully addressed to his daughter Laura, covers much the same ground as *Familiar Introduction to the History of Insects*. The insect world is described methodically and in detail. Wisely, Newman avoided rhyme altogether, thinking blank verse a more fitting a vehicle for the subject matter. Newman's love of insects shines through, though the reader may not agree with the sentiment, so passionately expressed, that earwigs are very beautiful to gaze on.

## Gnats

The true Gnats so bloodthirsty,
Gnats or Midges, CULICINA,
Mosquitoes of Culicina:
Males with feathery antennae,
Females with bloodsucking rostrum;
Both have heads of small dimensions;
Rather long and slender bodies,
Not nipped in or slender-waisted,
Legs are long and very slender.

In this country some few species
Of these Midges or Mosquitoes
Seek our faces in the night time:
With a gentle hum approaching
And an aperture creating
With their sharply pointed lancets,
Thence imbibe the purple current,
Causing us but slight annoyance.

## Earwigs

First of walkers come the Earwigs,
Earwigs or FORFICULINA;
The hind wings, quite transparent,
Like a lady's fan are folded

Neatly up beneath the fore wings,
And when opened out are earshaped,
Very beautiful to gaze on;
All the legs are very simple,
And the feet are all three jointed;
At the tail we find a weapon
Very like a pair of pincers,
And with this 'tis said the Earwigs
Open and fold up the hind wings;
You may watch them and observe it;
I have never had that pleasure.

## T. J. OUSELEY
## (fl. 1850s)

The theme of the next poem is the town of Douglas on
the Isle of Man, and the poet's style suggests that he was
more accustomed to prose than to verse. With this in
mind, one might expect the poem to be awful. One
would not be disappointed. In its defence, it can be said
that this is a commendably straightforward and
matter-of-fact poem; but I cannot imagine why anyone
would want to defend such an execrable work.

Castle Mona, says the poet, 'was erected fifty years
ago; / The cost exceeding forty thousand pounds'. The

town, however, 'boasts not architectural renown': the streets are 'narrow, crooked and unclean, / Ill paved, worst lighted,' despite of the protest emanating from some quarters. 'In fact,' he adds, 'there's nothing in them to be seen / But what is beggarly.' The same might be said for Ouseley's poems.

### Douglas, Isle of Man

Douglas again! The bay spreads wide its arms!
Near the broad sea proud Castle Mona stands,
A noble structure which has many charms,
Within a few yards of the level sands:
It is a princely mansion, and expands
Its wings of massive strength in stern array;
Its castellated form at once commands
The attention of the stranger on his way;
Magnificence and strength, the building both display.

It was erected fifty years ago;
The cost exceeding forty thousand pounds;
Near to its base the lake-like bay does flow;
There are delightful gardens; pleasure grounds,
And beauteous scenery the place surrounds;
With lovely shrubberies and choicest flowers,
This palace of a castle now abounds,
Here many 'mid the sylvan shades and bowers,
Retire to seek repose, and pass the joyous hours.

Such are sweet Nature's beauties. Of the town
The least 'tis possible to say were best;
It boasts not architectural renown,
Except the buildings on the hills that crest
The lovely bay; their bearing is due west:
The streets are narrow, crooked and unclean,
Ill paved, worst lighted – despite of protest;
In fact, there's nothing in them to be seen
But what is beggarly; in true parlance, they're mean.

# James Henry POWELL
# (fl. 1850)

Depression and mania are the twin qualities of James
Henry Powell's life and work. There is no oscillation
between the two; rather there is a slow progression from
the former to the latter. As a young man, he was a
pitiable and disconsolate wretch. His early poetry
inspires the same emotions in his readers. The first part
of his book of autobiography and verse, entitled *Life
Incidents and Poetic Pictures*, is a tale of aught but woe.
Rarely has such a bleak scene been painted in prose and
verse. The mood changes after Powell discovers poetry,
becoming ecstatic to an unnatural extreme.

## James Henry Powell

In the early part of his life, there was nothing about which he could be cheerful. Powell was born in 1830 to alcoholic parents in one of London's many slums. His childhood was one of poverty, unemployment, illness and injury, punctuated only by ill-timed deaths. Various relatives popped off to meet their Maker at awkward moments. Most importantly for our purposes, his friend's brother suffered an ignominious death, prompting the equally ignominious elegy below.

Death is a recurring theme in the book. Powell tells us that he escaped death on a number of occasions. We hear that he was almost crushed by a horse. He was nearly run over by a locomotive. He came very close to drowning. Most people, I suspect, would be cheerful to discover that they had slipped through the Grim Reaper's grasp. In Powell, however, near-death experiences caused only misery.

He grew up amidst poverty and dreamt of escaping to a suburb to live a mundane and bourgeois existence. He worked as an engineer, but he was sacked from every job he worked on. He tried working as a grocer, but a travelling pencil salesman took advantage of him and defrauded his business to the tune of a guinea. He tried to become a hypnotist but gave up when a vicar told him that his mouth was the wrong shape. Whatever line of business he entered, failure came with reliable rapidity.

Eventually, however, Powell heard the call of the

Muse. He turned to poetry for more for solace and consolation than for artistic ambitions. He exorcised the ghosts of his past through the medium of poetry. The poem below was written not to encourage drunkards to steer clear of railway lines but to put to rest Powell's demons. This is seen too in his other poems, most notably in 'The Dying Seamstress' and 'Idiot Bessie'.

Reinvigorated by this novel form of therapy, Powell staved off depression and avoided suicide, becoming at length quite cheerful. He was a changed man, forever smiling and laughing. He lectured at the Wolverton Mechanics' Institute on the subject of sunshine, flowers and songbirds. 'Who of us,' he asked his audience, 'has never heard the birdsong and felt the electric throbbing twang their heartstrings?'

**Lines Written for a Friend on the Death of his Brother, Caused by a Railway Train Running Over him whilst he was in a State of Inebriation**

How oft alas my brother have I warned thee to beware
The horrid spells of guilt which led the drunkard's
life to care;
But no! you heeded not the warning words I spoke
with pain,
Your wretched soul that once was pure was bound as

in a chain;
At length, one cold October, when the night was late
and dark,
The awful doom came on which sank thy life's
unsteady barque;
Thy mangled corpse upon the rails in frightful shape
was found,
The ponderous train had killed thee as its heavy
wheels went round;
And thus in dreadful form thou met'st a drunkard's
awful death,
And I, brother, mourn thy fate, and breathe a purer
breath.


## James Whitcomb RILEY
## (1846–1916)

The poetic career of James Whitcomb Riley is puzzling,
to say the least. Undoubtedly, Riley was a terrible poet.
His crude, ugly and ham-fisted poems are over-
sentimental in the extreme. His touch lacked sensitivity,
and his obsession with the Hoosier dialect is grating to
the modern ear. In the nineteenth century, however, Riley
was revered as America's best poet. Well-thumbed copies
of his books sat in every house, next to the Bible. The
royalties earned him a fortune. One can only conclude

that this was the most startling collective failure of taste ever to have been experienced by the people of America.

Riley was born in a log cabin in Greenfield, Indiana, in 1849. His father was a frontier lawyer and politician who named his second son after an Indiana governor, James Whitcomb. 'My father did not encourage my verse-making for he thought it too visionary,' said Riley, 'and being a visionary himself, he believed he understood the dangers of following the promptings of the poetic temperament.'

Riley left school at sixteen and travelled with a 'Miracle Medicine Show' as a musician, his task being to draw in the crowds so that the travelling quack could proceed to take advantage of the gullible audience. The poem 'Standard Remedies' dates from this period. Riley then worked as a journalist and his first published poems were written for newspapers. In 1872, his poetry appeared in *The Indianapolis Saturday Mirror*.

He moved to *The Indianapolis Journal*, and it was here that he first won acclaim for his work. It has been said that his sentimental style 'harkened back to simpler times and struck a chord with a reading public struggling to come to grips with the industrial age.' It reads more as if it struck a chord with an industrial public struggling to come to grips with reading.

Either way, Riley became one of the best-loved poets in America. Upon his death in 1916, more than 35,000 people filed past his casket as it lay in state under the dome at the Indiana State Capitol. President Woodrow Wilson sent a note of sorrow to Riley's family. 'With his departure,' wrote Wilson, 'a notable figure passes out of the nation's life; a man who imparted joyful pleasure and a thoughtful view of many things that other men would have missed.'

The pandering to public taste was the cause of Riley's fame. It is also the root of his failure as a poet. Riley himself came close to admitting this. 'The public,' he wrote, 'desires nothing but what is absolutely natural, and so perfectly natural as to be fairly artless. It cannot tolerate affectation, and it takes little interest in the classical production. It demands simple sentiments.' In order to better define the tastes of the masses, Riley gave public readings of his poems in order to gauge the response:

'While on the lecture platform, I watched the effect that my readings had on the audience very closely and whenever anybody left the hall I knew that my recitation was at fault and tried to find out why. Once a man and his wife made an exit while I was giving "The Happy Little Cripple" – a recitation I had prepared with particular enthusiasm and satisfaction. It fulfilled, as few poems do, all the requirements of length, climax and those many necessary features for a recitation. The subject was a theme of real pathos, beautified by the cheer and optimism of the little sufferer. Consequently when this couple left the hall I was very anxious to know the reason and asked a friend to find out. He learned that they had a little hunchback child of their own. After this experience I never used that recitation again.'

### Standard Remedies

Wherever blooms of health are blown,
McCrillus' Remedies are known;
Wherever happy lives are found
You'll find his medicines around,
From coughs and colds and lung disease
His patients find a sweet release
In using his Expectorant
That cures where even doctors can't.
His Oriental Liniment
Is known to fame to such extent
That orders for it emanate
From every portion of the State,
His European Balsam, too,
Send blessings down to me and you;
And holds its throne from year to year
In every household far and near,
His purifier for the blood
Has earned a name fair and good
As ever glistened on the page
Of any annals of the age.

And he who pants for health ease
Should try these Standard Remedies.

*From* **The Little Hunchback**

I'm nine years old! an' you can't guess how much I
weigh, I bet!
Last birthday I weighed thirty-three! An' I weigh
thirty yet!
I'm awful little for my size – I'm purt' nigh littler 'an
Some babies is! – an' neighbours all calls me "The
Little Man!"
An' Doc one time he laughed and said: "I 'spect, first
thing you know,
You'll have a spike-tail coat an' travel with a show!"
An' nen I laughed – till I looked round an' Aunty was
a cryin' –
Sometimes she acts like that, 'cause I got "curv'ture of
the spine!"

# Amanda McKittrick ROS
# (1860–1939)

In the 1890s, Amanda McKittrick Ros began publishing
decidedly old-fashioned novels about romance, chivalry

and decency. They all bear intriguingly alliterative titles, such as *Donald Dudley* and *Irene Iddesleigh*. The latter contains one of the best lines of prose ever written:

'Speak! Irene! Wife! Woman! Do not sit in silence and allow the blood that now boils in my veins to ooze through cavities of unrestrained passion and trickle down to drench me with its crimson hue!'

Her second novel, *Delina Delaney*, begins with a singularly incomprehensible question:

'Have you ever visited that portion of Erin's plot that offers its sympathetic soil for the minute survey and scrutinous examination of those in political power, whose decision has wisely been the means before now of converting the stern and prejudiced, and reaching the hand of slight aid to share its strength in augmenting its agricultural richness?'

The novels were followed by Ros's alliteratively titled books of verse: *Poems of Puncture* was followed by *Fumes of Formation*. The latter, Ross explains, was 'hatched within a mind fringed with Fumes of Formation, the Ingenious Innings of Inspiration and Thorny Tincture of Thought.'

'My chief object in writing,' she wrote, 'is and always has been to write if possible in a strain all my own. My works are all expressly my own – pleasingly peculiar –

not a borrowed stroke in one of them.' Aldous Huxley saw through the pretence and summed up her works as mannered and contrived: 'The first attempts of any people to be consciously literary,' he said, 'are always productive of the most elaborate artificiality.'

Ros was as socially aspirational in life as she was in literature. She changed her name from 'Ross' to 'Ros' in order to suggest that she was part of the ancient de Ros family and claimed that the McKittricks were descended from King Sitric of Denmark.

### From On Visiting Westminster Abbey

Holy Moses! Have a look!
Flesh decayed in every nook!
Some rare bits of brain lie here
Mortal loads of beef and beer,
Some of whom are turned to dust,
Every one bids lost to lust;
Royal flesh so tinged with 'blue'
Undergoes the same as you.
Wealth and lands were theirs to boast,
Yachts lying nigh to every coast,
Homage from the million theirs
Clad in gold and gorgeous wares.
Here they lie who had such store,
Move a muscle – nevermore;

Dead as all before them died:
Richer man are you beside,
Begging as you walk your way,
Life still yours while dead are they:
All the refuse lying here
Has no life to give it cheer.
Alas! You stand above them all
Tho' poverty did you befall.
Life was fine, once noble lord!
Now you tramp on their record.
Tributes of 'Masonic Love'
Shall not passports prove Above.
Slabs of monumental art
Tell the sycophants' remarks.
Noble once, these dead folk now,
Darkness stamped have on their brow.
All portrays without – within
Lots of love and shoals of sin.
Famous some were – yet they died:
Poets – Statesmen – Rogues beside,
Kings – Queens, all of them do rot,
What about them? Now – they're not!

# Francis Saltus SALTUS
## (1849–1889)

Francis Saltus Saltus is one of poetry's many unintentionally hilarious characters. An American by nationality, he tried to reinvent himself as a fin-de-siècle European Decadent. Affectation and pretence were not skills at which he excelled. The sham was immediately apparent. He was not debauched. He was not depraved. He was not dissolute. He was a fake, and everyone knew it. He stuck to his guns, however, becoming increasingly ridiculous in his overdramatic and exaggerated pose.

I am not the first person to notice the striking resemblance between Francis Saltus Saltus and the fictional character Enoch Soames in Max Beerbohm's short story of the same name. Soames, who hails from Preston, is a would-be Decadent poet who fails to convince. He writes collections of poems with names like 'Fungoids' and sinks into absurdity.

I am convinced that Beerbohm based his fictional character on Francis Saltus Saltus. The similarities are too numerous to be mere coincidences. Most striking is the physical resemblance between the two men. Beerbohm describes Soames as being 'very pale, with longish and brownish hair. He had a thin vague beard — or rather, he had a chin on which a large number of hairs weakly curled and clustered to cover its retreat. He was an odd-looking person ... He wore a soft black hat of the clerical kind but of Bohemian intention, and a grey waterproof cape, which, perhaps because it was waterproof, failed to be romantic'. The frontispiece to one of Saltus's books is a lithograph of a man fitting this description precisely. In the picture, Saltus wears a small black hat of the clerical kind.

Saltus wrote over five thousand poems before he died at thirty-nine, but, like Soames in Beerbohm's story, he failed to achieve fame. He wrote innumerable poems about alcohol in a series called *Flasks and Flagons*, which included the mandatory poems about absinthe, the decadent's drink of choice. His other poems return frequently to the obligatory and predictable themes of the Decadent movement: femmes fatales, sadism, masochism, morbidity, perverse religiosity, madness and more absinthe. 'He works his way conscientiously through the characters and situations of decadence,' writes one commentator, 'as if ticking them off on a mental list.'

'Although he idealised cigarette-smoking women, looked for pornography in the Bible, and honoured Baudelaire, Gérard de Nerval and the Marquis de Sade,' wrote another scholar, 'he never escaped the tone of a boy who expected any moment to be caught smoking behind the barn.'

## To a Scrap of Sea Weed

Neglected flower that in the ocean blooms,
Poor exile from the fragrant groves of earth,
What sorrow rises in thy salt perfumes,
To what sad thoughts thy humble charm gives birth!

Tosses by the tempest and fluctuant tide,
The vulgar plaything of the slimy eel;
Crushed by the vessel's keel or cast aside,
What bitterness thy injured heart must feel!

Thy lovely sisters blush on field and lawn,
The lily, pink and rose are kin to thee,
Yet thou art destined, from grim night till dawn,
To hide thy envy in the turbulent sea.

Alas! none know why thou wast strangely torn
From leafy woodlands and rich orchards blest,
Nor why thou shouldst not have been sweetly born
A tuberose to grace my darling's breast,

Unless the Eternal, in His august might,
A sacred usage for thy beauty found,
And made thee to fulfil some sacred rite
Upon the ghastly foreheads of the drowned.

# J. B. SMILEY
## (fl. 1880s)

Bad poets are ignored by their contemporaries. They are not lauded by their peers. They receive little attention from the public. They slip, unnoticed, from the pages of history. As a result, the scholar of bad verse faces a difficult task. Reliable biographical information is hard to find. The records are at best sparse and at worst non-existent. It is tempting in such circumstances to engage in the nefarious practice of fabrication. The honourable and praiseworthy course of action, however, is the admittance of defeat. It must be said at this juncture that J. B. Smiley has defeated me. I have been able to discover few significant facts about his life.

I know only that he published two volumes of verse. The first, called *Meditations of Samuel Wilkins*, was published in 1886. The second, *A Basket of Chips*, was published in 1888. Regrettably I have not been able to get my hands on a copy of either book. The British Library does not possess anything by J. B. Smiley. It was a grave disappointment to discover that the Bodleian also lacked the volumes in question.

I have found only two poems by the man himself. I am confident that the extracts below are accurate, as my source was reliable. They are pretty awful, which makes things all the more infuriating. I am keen to discover more of Smiley's verse, but I fear that it has all been submerged beneath the tide of time. Anyone who is able to find anything of any relevance will be handsomely rewarded with a bag of fruit pastilles. In the meantime, however, and unless and until some momentous discovery is made, the poems below will remain the only extant verses by J. B. Smiley.

### *From* Beautiful Spring

The north winds are still and the blizzards at rest,
All in the beautiful spring.
The dear little robins are building their nests,
All in the beautiful spring.
The tramp appears and for lodging begs,
The old hen sitteth on turkey eggs,
And the horse has scratches in all four legs,
All in the beautiful spring.

### Kalamazoo

On the outskirts are celery marshes
Which only a few years ago
Were as wet as a drugstore in Kansas
And as worthless as marshes could grow,
Well some genius bethought him to drain them
And to add in a short year or two

About eighty-five thousand dollars
To the income of Kalamazoo.

The Michigan Insane Asylum
Is up on the top of the hill,
And some irresponsible crazies
Meander around there at will,
And they frequently talk to a stranger,
And they sometimes escape, it is true,
But the folks are not all of them crazy
Who hail from Kalamazoo.

# Horace SMITH
## (fl. 1860s)

Horace Smith must be commended for his fine sense of
the dramatic and his preternatural ability to add startling
and altogether unexpected endings to his poems. Within
the space of a few lines, the protagonist's fortunes change
without warning, illuminating what may only be called
the vicissitudes of life.

### Disappointment

Joy! joy! my lover's bark returns,
I know her by her bearing brave:
How gallantly the foam she spurns,
And bounds in triumph o'er the wave!

Why dost thou veil the glorious sight,
In lurid rain, thou summer cloud?
See! see! the lightning flashes bright!
Hark! to the thunder long and loud!

The storm is past — the skies are fair,
But where's the bark? — she was but one —
Ha! she is yonder, shatter'd — bare —
She reels — she — sinks — O Heaven! she's gone!

## William B. TAPPAN
## (1794–1849)

The Reverend William B. Tappan of Boston wrote over
twelve volumes of poetry whilst working for the
American Sunday School Union. One critic has written
that Tappan's poems 'are all of unflagging moral
rectitude commingled with enthusiastic, even bouncy,

zeal'. This is true of the greater part of his poems. It is true that he was prone to sermonising, and he did write many verses about the evils of drink. But it is not true of all of his poems, as the verse below demonstrates. Never before or since has the tomato been so jubilantly celebrated in verse. It is taken from a volume entitled *Sacred and Miscellaneous Poems*, which was published 1847. Presumably this comes under the heading 'Miscellaneous'.

### The Tomato

Tomato! thou art like the mind
That moves not feebly with mankind;
Who loves thee, give a generous part,
Who hate thee, hate with all the heart.

My morsel good, my table neat,
I am not anxious what I eat;
If she, whose smile is always glad,
Lights up the mean, 'tis never bad.

I have my favourite, as have most,
Among the baked, and boiled, and roast;
Yet, for my tit-bit, would not go
To farther clime than Mexico.

## William B. Tappan

To Mexico! – I give him praise
Who, hither, from those unknown ways,
And barbarous men, of Spanish breed,
Conveyed the small Tomato seed.

Sure, with his lion-heart and skill,
He might have sacked her mines at will –
But Mexico's chief wealth to take!
I'll love Tomato for his sake.

And for thine own, celestial Fruit!
(Not vegetable,) made to suit
All circumstances; or to pluck
And eat, as I in Old Kentuck

Have done; or with white sugar sliced,
Or soused in vinegar, well spiced,
Or smothered in the pie, or stewed,
Which I like best. Thou art of food

The simplest, sweetest, richest, best.
O, had my humble verses zest
Half as delicious as thine own,
From Byron, Burns, I'd take the throne,

Superior in artistic pride
As thou to edibles beside!

I see from earth thy tendril peep,
And on its bosom try to creep,

Till, propped secure, it stands upright,
And brings its tiny germs to light.
I see thee on the laden bush,
(Not to excess my verse to push,)

In thy first coat of emerald green,
That soon a brilliant scarlet's seen;
I see thee gathered, scalded, skinned –
Some care in stripping off thy rind –

Then duly cut, by practice, nice,
In pieces small, and in a trice,
With rites of salt and butter paid –
In sauce-pan buried, and o'erlaid

With cover; that the steaming tin
The needful heat may keep within;
Soon done – ye fair! The bowl produce,
And fill it with the pulp and juice;

And now – with bread (or toast) and tea,
Nought else – a feast for princes see!
For princes? Mouth of King Phillipe,
Or dame Victoria's pretty lip,

Hath bliss beyond a monarch's lacked,
If neither hath Tomato smacked.
Not fruit the lovely Houri sees,
Not apple of Hesperides,

Not cantaloupe, or luscious grape,
Not pear of bell, or other shape,
Not melon, of red juicy ore,
No coconut, of milky store,

Not dishes of a thousand lands,
To fatten cooks and kill gourmands,
Westphalian ham, Bohemian boar
Or haggis, which the Scotch adore;

"Ros bif" of England, Frenchman's frog,
Or Sandwich Island hog or dog,
Nor all that gastronomic scroll,
Though Epicurus called the roll,

Or horticultural art can show
May, with the pride of Mexico –
"Quick! quick! sure, husband, love, you're heady,
D'ye hear? leave off! Tomato's ready!"

# Frederick THOMAS
## (fl. 1870s)

Teignmouth, apparently, was beautified in the 1870s. Frederick Thomas wrote a poem to celebrate the improvements. 'I take off my hat,' says the poet, 'to all who laboured to accomplish that.' But not all is well. Thomas is alarmed by the recent sale and imminent deconstruction of Teignmouth pier. The pier, says the poet, 'helps to beautify / This charming watering-place'. Soon, however, it will be gone. 'I scarcely believe what I am told,' says the poet in mild amazement. He is, however, opposed to the charging of a toll for access to the pier, however small it may be, for a toll is 'clearly a short-sighted policy'.

### Teignmouth

Who can on Teignmouth look, and not exclaim,
'Why, is it possible that 'tis the same!'
And yet the strange old church looks just as when
I saw it last.
Surely this promenade, this lovely green,
This handsome place which I today have seen,
Marks not the spot where one could scarcely stand
Without both eyes and boots being filled with sand.
And yet it is; so I take off my hat

To all who laboured to accomplish that.
And yonder pier, too, helps to beautify
This charming watering-place — though, by-the-bye,
I scarcely believe what I am told,
That soon 'twill be removed — in fact, 'is sold'.

And I believe to charge, however small
The toll for access to the pier may be,
Is clearly a short-sighted policy;
For looking round about, who can deny,
As all that's truly charming meets the eye,
That old Dame Nature had with lavish grace
Been generous to this lovely watering-place?
A splendid space of sea we here behold,
On either hand the coast stands clear and bold,
Whilst in the background, sheltered and serene,
Are cosy villas looking o'er the scene.

## Martin Farquhar TUPPER (1810–1889)

During Martin Tupper's lifetime, his name inspired two
very different reactions in two very different sets of
people. One set of people thought his poetry was
wonderful. His books sold in large numbers. By the

1860s his first volume of verse had sold over half a million copies worldwide. 'I thank you, Mr Tupper, for your beautiful poetry,' wrote Queen Victoria to the poet in 1857. With the benefit of hindsight, it safe to say that Tupper's admirers had exceedingly bad taste.

The other set of people, including almost all of the poetry reviewers, detested Tupper and everything he stood for. One contemporary critic described Tupper's verse as 'rivulets of treacle,' and another called it 'incredible rubbish and intolerable imbecility'.

Posterity has tended to side with the detractors. The *Dictionary of National Biography* says of his verse that 'the style, with its queer inversions, bears more resemblance to the English of an erudite German of the nineteenth century'. *Everyman's Dictionary of Literary Biography* says that his first book is 'a singular collection of commonplace observations set forth in a form which bears the appearance of verse, but has neither rhyme nor metre, and has long since found its deserved level'.

The following poem is a rallying call for white Anglo-Saxon Protestants. It exhorts them to colonise the furthest reaches of the habitable globe. Imperialism in most vulgar and jingoistic form sounds odd to modern ears, to say the least. The poet announces that the global dominance of Anglo-Saxon genes is imminent: 'Feebly dwindling day by day, / All other races are fading away'.

## The Anglo-Saxon Race: A Rhyme for Englishmen

Stretch forth! stretch forth! from the south to the
north!
From the east to the west, stretch forth! stretch forth!
Strengthen thy stakes, and lengthen thy cords,
The world is a tent for the world's true lords!
Break forth and spread over every place,
The world is a world for the Saxon Race!

England sowed the glorious seed,
In her wise old laws, and her pure old creed,
And her stout old heart, and her plain old tongue,
And her resolute energies, ever young,
And her free bold hand, and her frank fair face,
And her faith in the rule of the Saxon Race!

Feebly dwindling day by day,
All other races are fading away;
The sensual South, and the servile East,
And the tottering throne of the treacherous priest,
And every land is in evil case
But the wide scatter'd realm of the Saxon Race!

Englishmen everywhere! brethren all!
By one great name on your millions I call,
Norman, American, Gael, and Celt,

Into this fine mixed mass ye melt,
And all the best of your best I trace
In the golden brass of the Saxon Race!

Englishmen everywhere! faithful and free!
Lords of the land, and kings of the sea,
Anglo-Saxons! honest and true,
By hundreds of millions my word is to you,
Love one another! as brothers embrace!
That the world may be blest in the Saxon Race!

## Samuel WESLEY
## (1660–1735)

The Methodist movement has been keen to forget about Samuel Wesley's poetry. It has often been stated that most of Samuel's work was lost in a fire at Epworth. Fortunately, this is not true. Samuel's most important work, the gracefully entitled *Maggots: Or, Poems On Several Subjects Never Before Handled*, can be found in the British Library. Upon reading 'Maggots', it becomes immediately obvious why the Methodist movement would rather Samuel Wesley's poetry didn't exist. John Wesley's father was a terrible poet.

The work, published in 1685, does indeed contain

poems on subjects never before handled. The ambition of the subject matter is impressive. The grunting of pigs and suppers of stinking ducks are rendered in verse alongside poems entitled 'Three Skips of a Louse' and 'On the Bear-Fac'd Lady'. The frontispiece carries an engraving of the poet with a generously proportioned maggot positioned on his brow, but in fact the title poem on maggots is one of the least adventurous.

The most noticeable feature of Samuel Wesley's poetry is the distinctive tone. His poems are boisterous, roistering, energetic and bawdy. One thinks immediately of ruddy cheeks, flea infestations, gallons of sour port and drunken brawls in malodorous alehouses.

Only Samuel Wesley could have written of the ducks he ate for dinner: 'They dropp'd from the Moon out of Breath, and the Thumps / Which they took on the Ground have discolour'd their Rumps'. Only Samuel Wesley could have written of a woman who insulted him: 'E'en get a Mask, or with thy Visage daunted, / The Londoners will swear their Streets are haunted'. As a poet, Samuel Wesley was one of a kind.

## A Pindaricque, On the Grunting of a Hog

Freeborn Pindaric never does refuse,
Either a lofty, or a humble Muse:
Now in proud Sophoclaeligan Buskins Sings,
Of Hero's, and of Kings,
Mighty Numbers, mighty Things;
Now out of sight she flys,
Rowing with gaudy Wings
Across the stormy Skys,
Then down again,
Her self she Flings,
Without uneasiness, or Pain
To Lice, and Dogs,
To Cows, and Hogs,
And follows their melodious grunting o'er the Plain.

Harmonious Hog draw near!
No bloody Butchers here,
Thou need'st not fear,
Harmonious Hog draw near, and from thy beauteous
                                        Snowt
Whilst we attend with Ear,
Like thine prick'd up devout;
To taste thy Sug'ry voice, which here, and there,
With wanton Curls, vibrates around the circling Air,
Harmonious Hog! warble some Anthem out!

As sweet as those which quiv'ring Monks in days of
                                                Yore,
With us did roar;
When they alas,
That the hard-hearted Abbot such a Coyl should
                                                keep,
And cheat 'em of their first, their sweetest Sleep;
When they were ferreted up to Midnight Mass:
Why should not other Piggs on Organs play,
As well as They.

Dear Hog! thou King of Meat!
So near thy Lord Mankind,
The nicest Taste can scarce a difference find!
No more may I thy glorious Gammons eat!
No more,
Partake of the Free Farmers Christmass store,
Black Puddings which with Fat would make your
        Mouths run o'er:
If I, tho' I should ne'er so long before the Sentence
                                                stay,
And in my large Ears scale, the thing ne'er so dis
                                                creetly weigh,
If I can find a difference in the Notes,
Belcht from the applauded Throats
Of Rotten Play house Songsters-All-Divine,
If any difference I can find between their Notes, and
                                                Thine:

A Noise they keep with Tune, and out of Tune,
And Round, and Flat,
High, Low, and This, and That,
That Algebra, or Thou, or I might understand as
soon.

Like the confounding Lutes innumerable Strings,
One of them Sings;
Thy easier Musick's ten times more divine;
More like the one string'd, deep, Majestick Trump-
Marine:
Prythee strike up, and cheer this drooping Heart of
Mine!
Not the sweet Harp that's claim'd by Jews,
Nor that which to the far more Ancient Welch
belongs,
Nor that which the Wild Irish use,
Frighting even their own Wolves with loud
Hubbubbaboos.
Nor Indian Dance, with Indian Songs, Nor yet,
(Which how should I so long forget?)
The Crown of all the rest,
The very Cream o' th' Jest:
Amptuous Noble Lyre-the Tongs;
Nor, tho' Poetick Jordan bite his Thumbs,
At the bold word, my Lord Mayors Flutes, and Kettle-
Drums;

Not all this Instrumental dare,
With thy soft, ravishing, vocal Musick ever to compare.

## On a Supper of Stinking Ducks

The story thus – At a Clubb of Younkers, after a Frost a
couple of Wild-Ducks were bought. A thaw
coming the day after, these having before been frozen hard,
fell in, appeared all black, and stunk most
harmoniously – yet, that nothing good might be
wasted, the Purchasers dressed 'em, and eat the first pretty
nimbly, not staying to taste it; but by that time, Colon being
a little pacified, advancing to the second, it drove 'em all
off, and was given a decent burial at last in the Boghouse.

At the place that you wot of hight Clerken-well-
                                          Green!
First of all Merry Mac, come and taste our good
                                          cheer,
For our Hearts will all vibrate thy Lyricks to hear.
One and all run and Saddle your Cane, or your Beast,
And hasten full speed to the bountiful Feast!
In pow'rful Gambado's, or sinical Boot;
In a thrid-bare old Cloak, or a new Sur le tout!
Or flaming with Fringe, or meek Kid on your Hand,
With blustering Cravat, or reverent Band!
Both peaceable Hazle, and Kill-devil Steel,
Both Tory-Bamboo, and Fanatick-Brazeel!

# The World's Worst Poetry

Remember Batts Axiom, your Curtlass prepare!
Whet Stomachs, and Knives! Here's a Bill of the Fare;

Here's Duck upon Duck, for no more you must look;
If you'll have any more you must go to the Cook.
I tell you the Truth, and I tell you no lie!
They shine and 'twere Butter, or Stars in the Sky:
Zich glorry-vatt Ducks but zildom are zean,
Whore shou'd they be bore but about Taunton-Dean.
If they stink Mrs. Muse your nice Nose you may
                                                    hold!
Disparage 'em not for they're bought, and they're sold;
Consider as cheap of the Poulter they had 'em,
As e'er of the Higler — (the Servant!)
Here Dick, Black-Bess for thy absence should frown,
Look over thy Shoulder, and 'tweak off their Down:
But prythee deal gently, for 'twould be no Wonder,
They're so soft, and so young, if they fall all-asunder.
'Tis true I confess, if my Nostrils can tell,
They send out a kind of a Civity smell:
Yet more then a Bustard the Poulter might prize one
Like them, for their flavour like pasty Venizon.

Some will say they've a whiff like a Worm-eaten Bitch,
Or a Tartar Ragoo, ready dress'd in a Ditch:
Or a cleanly blue-Pig — but ne'er keck honest fellow!
For they're wholesome enow, tho' a little too mellow.

Samuel Wesley

They're black, but where Indians do paint the Devil
                                        White,
That colour be sure's a most heavenly sight:
They dropp'd from the Moon out of Breath, and the
                                        Thumps
Which they took on the Ground have discolour'd
                                        their Rumps.
Cozen John! 't had been better if y'had not been so
                                        sickle,
But in our Garden-Cellar had laid 'em in pickle:
Tho' the Cook says they're sweet, I'll venture engage
                                        her,
That the Ducks should ha' stunk with the T--'s for a
                                        Wager.
Pothecary's Bills have full often half broke us,
With chargeable Vomits of Carduus and Crocus:
When these Ducks from the Bum-gut to Keckhorn
                                        would draw,
And like a Turn'd-Pudding-bag empty the Maw;
O Spirits of Arm-pits, and Essence of Toes!
O Hogo of Ulcers, and Hospital Nose!

O Devils Dung fragant, and tarrifi'd feather,
With Snuff, and with Carrion, Ana, jumbled together!
O Jelly of Toads! India's hasty-Pudding!
O Playsters of Issues champt down o'the sudden!
With fat blubby Pease, that are grimy all o'er,

Thick butter'd with delicate matter and Gore!
Well! If these you survive, I'll believe 'tis no Fable,
That Indians gut Adders, and bring 'em to Table:
But after, if your Pest'lent Breath sally on us,
We'll get to the Windward, or Mercy upon us!
Hoyst 'em up with a Rope at the Fire! 'tis no matter,
Tho' they drop in the dripping, and crawl in the
                                            Platter;
So do's the sweet Phaenix on Frankincense-Faggot,
Sit roasting her self till she turn to a Maggot.

## On a Discourteous Damsel that call'd the Right Worshipful Author (an't please ye!) Sawcy Puppy

Ugly! ill-natur'd! impudent, and proud!
Sluttish! nonsensical! and idly loud!
Thy Name's a ranker Scandal to my Pen,
Than all thy words could be spew'd up agen.
Yet will I do thy Ugliness the grace,
To touch thee, tho' I'm forc'd to turn my face;
Touch thee as Surgeon touches rotten sores,
Touch thee as Nurses T--, or Beadles Whores.

Belch of a Toad whom Hell to Mortals sends,
Vampt up from Bottle-Ale and Candles-ends.
Hadst thou no Dick with whom thou mightst be free,
Thus to let fly thy Whetstone-jeers on me?
What Skip-kennel without his eyes offence,

Taught thee all this Dog-and-bitch Eloquence?
Thou for Doll Troop, hadst ended Ragoo's strife,
He'd hang'd, and never ventur'd such a Wife.

That thick deformity which daubs thy Snowt
Would make a Hell-soul'd Ravisher devout.
An Incubus from such a Face would flee;
'Twould baulk a Satyr more deform'd than thee.
E'en get a Mask, or with thy Visage daunted,
The Londoners will swear their Streets are haunted:
Below the Plague, below the Pox and Itch,
Take your own Farewell, You're a sawcy Bitch.

# Cornelius WHUR
## (1782–1853)

Men of the cloth, on the whole, are not good poets. So practised are they at propounding the Word to their flocks that their style is frequently the same on the page as it is in the pulpit. Their poems can be moralistic and didactic. Sermonising, it is fair to say, is not well suited to verse. All denominations are alike in this. Vicars, preachers and priests should not dabble in rhyme.

The Reverend Cornelius Whur is an exception to this rule. His poetry is too bad to be ignored. It is not dull. No one can say that it is patronising. To read Cornelius

Whur's verse is to experience a close encounter with borderline insanity. Whur's madness, it must be said, is madness of the most entertaining kind. His mildly irrational obsession with the physically disabled is only one of the unusual traits to be found in his work. The inappropriate use of exclamation marks displays a certain maniacal animation. It is, I fear, enough to alarm the frail. At every turn, the absurd lurks behind the commonplace.

Whur was a Wesleyan minister who lived in Norfolk. His first volume of verse, entitled *Village Musings on Moral and Religious Subjects*, was published in 1837. It must have been popular with his congregation, as it went through three editions. Such was public demand for more of the same that he produced a second book, called *Gratitude's Offering*, in 1845.

As can be seen from the verses below, Whur was keen to preface his poems with introductory paragraphs in which he explains, so that no confusion may arise in the minds of his readers, the behind-the-scenes goings-on and the thought processes that culminated in the writing of the poem in question. Often he explains the meaning of the poem itself. Occasionally the poem adds little to the introductory paragraph, repeating in verse what has been said with greater clarity in prose. As a result of these helpful prefaces from the poet himself, the poems below need nothing by way of explanation.

## *From* The Cheerful Invalid

The following lines refer to a Lady who has passed the last 14 years of her life without walking, having been principally confined to her bed during that extended period, except for four or five hours at the close of each day; and for that change of scene is entirely indebted to the assistance of her attendants. The lady, notwithstanding this privation, is so resigned to her melancholy situation, as to present an admirable picture of contentment and resignation to the Divine will. The writer had the pleasure of spending two evenings in the company of the lady, and in the concluding verses expresses the deep submission which was displayed by the sufferer, and which, he is happy to add, is uniformly evinced.

Dost thou not feel as years recede,
Worn out, distressed and weary?
To me, it seemeth, thou hast need,
To be from sorrow's pelting freed,
In such a state – so dreary.
Year after year, thou art the same,
An invalid – remaining lame!

## *From* The Laborious Ants

The following lines were occasioned by the author's seeing a perforated piece of wood, in the shop of a watchmaker, which had been taken out of an ant's nest; and which, by their astonishing labour, had been reduced to a state very much resembling the combs ordinarily seen in the hives of bees.

Why did you, feeble as you were, attempt
A task, so perfectly Herculean?
Could it be to rear your tender offspring?
Did your concern touching their welfare
So impel? Was aught like conference held
Ere you began to calculate success?
Could you foresee the toil awaiting you?
Month's receding, must have left you lab'ring
Short of wished-for issue! Incessant
Toil alone produced such perforations!
Intrepid ants! your prowess I admire,
However I may fail in copying you.

### *From* To a Little Girl

The following lines apply to a little girl who was born without either legs or arms, and who (of course) is altogether dependent upon her parents under all circumstances.

Why art thou child, famed for imperfection,
Happily rejoicing? Canst thou see aught
Before thy face but want approaching thee?
Not having legs or arms how wilt thou play

Thy part, or act life's drama? Thy loved ones
Fondly cleaving so, will ere long leave thee;
Nor sooth as now thy tender, loving heart –
Relieving all thy wants. Then, undefended,
To whom wilt thou repair – mercy asking?
Thou wilt, I fear, find friends a rarity!

*From* The Rose-Covered Grave

The Author, in passing through a beautiful
churchyard in the county of Norfolk, was particularly
struck with the appearance of a recently covered grave,
which was surrounded by a profusion of roses. Afterwards,
while proceeding on his journey, he casually overtook the
gentleman whose lady had been interred in the grave which
had engaged his attention; and of whose sudden departure
he gave the following relation. He had an only daughter,
who at the period referred to, was seriously indisposed, and
who had been deploring that circumstance inconsequence
of the inconvenience it occasioned in the family. The lady,
who at that time was in perfect health, endeavoured to
console the mind of her afflicted daughter, by exclaiming,
"Thank God, I am quite well, and will alleviate your
sufferings!" But within twenty minutes, the affectionate
mother, who had thus spoken, was a corpse; and in the
above-named grave her remains were reposing.

The morning arose, and its beauties were beaming,
As they danced in her vision like snow-crested wave;

But alas! as such splendours were brilliantly gleaming,
She retired to repose in the rose-covered grave!

## *From* The Armless Artist

The lines below were suggested by seeing an artist who was
born without arms, who supports himself and his parents
also, by his profession.

'Alas! alas!' the father said,
'O what a dispensation!
How can we be by mercy led,
In such a situation?
Be not surprised by my alarms,
The dearest boy is without arms!

 'I have no hope, nor confidence,
The scene around is dreary;
How can I meet such vast expense?
I am by trying, weary.
You must, my dearest, plainly see,
This armless boy will ruin me.'

# Ella Wheeler WILCOX
## (1850–1919)

Ella Wheeler Wilcox was a farm girl from Wisconsin with literary ambitions and a firm belief in teetotalism. She was very popular with the temperance movement, the members of which must have read her poems not to reinforce their abstinence but to relish the self-satisfied and righteous tone that pervaded her work. Her poems are also characterised by a galling sentimentality and the nauseating veneration of 'practical common sense'.

### Alcohol's Requiem Upon Prof. P. F. K., A Gifted Man, Who Died A Victim To Strong Drink

Ho! ho! Father Death! I have won you another!
Another grand soul I have ruined and taken;
I, who am licensed by good Christian people,
Eat and eat at their souls till by angels forsaken:
I spoil them, I soil them, and past all reclaiming
They fall, sick with sins that are too black for naming.

Ho! ho! Father Death! count me as your best man:
I bring you more souls than famine or battle.
Let pestilence rage! it will last but a season,
And the soft voice of peace stills the cannon's loud
                                    rattle;

But I, pausing never, with ceaseless endeavor,
Night and day, day and night, I am toiling for ever.

Ho! ho! Father Death! I have brought you my thou
sands:
Good people help me, license, uphold me,
Gaze on some victim I stole from their household –
Gaze, and upbraid the foul demon that sold me.
Ah! but they helped him – argued and voted
Till license was granted, and I was promoted.


Ho! ho! Father Death! is he not a grand victim?
I bring you souls that are well worth the winning –
Noble and brave, with the rare gifts of heaven;
But I eat them away and pollute them with sinning.
Now, but for me there would be few above him,
Honoured and prized by the dear ones who love him.

## Don't Drink

Don't drink, boys, don't!
There is nothing of happiness, pleasure, or cheer,
In brandy, in whiskey, in rum, ale, or beer.
If they cheer you when drunk, you are certain to pay
In headaches and crossness the following day.
Don't drink, boys, don't!

Boys, let it alone!
Turn your back on your deadliest enemy – Drink!
An assassin disguised; nor for one moment think,
As some rashly say, that true women admire
The man who can boast that he's playing with fire.
Boys, let it alone!
No, boys, don't drink!

If the habit's begun, stop now! stop to-day!
Ere the spirit of thirst leads you on and away
Into vice, shame, and drunkenness. This is the goal,
Where the spirit of thirst leads the slave of the bowl.
No, boys, don't drink!
Boys, touch not, nor taste!

Don't think you can stop at the social 'First Glass'.
Too many have boasted that power, alas!
And found they were slaves to this seeming good
                                        friend,
And have grown into drunkards and knaves, in the
                                        end.

Boys, touch not, nor taste!
Don't drink, boys, Don't!

If the loafers and idlers scoff, never heed:
True men and true women will wish you "God-
                                        speed".

**189**

There is nothing of purity, pleasure, or cheer
To be gotten from whiskey, wine, brandy, or beer.
Don't drink, boys, Don't!

## *From* When Baby Souls Sail Out

When a child goes yonder
And leaves its mother here,
Its little feet must wander,
It seems to me, in fear.

It must be when the baby
Goes journeying off alone,
Some angel (Mary maybe),
Adopts it for her own.

Yet when a child is taken
Whose mother stays below
With weeping eyes, through Paradise,
I seem to see it go.

With troops of angels trying
To drive away its fear,
I seem to hear it crying
"I want my mamma here."

I do not court the fancy,
It is not based on doubt,

It is a thought that comes unsought
When baby souls sail out.


# George Joseph WILLIAMSON
# (b. 1816)

George Joseph Williamson was born at Rochester in
1816. As befitted the son of a ship-owner, he was sent
to sea as a young boy. Almost every ship he set foot on
was soon shipwrecked, and Williamson, forced to swim
for his life on a weekly basis, was soon inured to the
dangers of life at sea.

Lady Luck was perhaps smiling on him, for he was
certainly more fortunate that his fellow sailors. 'Out of
twelve acquaintances during my apprenticeship,' he
wrote, 'six were drowned, three met with sad ends, one
was crushed between two ships, and another died covered
with vermin.'

It is no surprise that he preferred to stay on dry land,
pen in hand, writing poems about the cruel sea. The
ocean-faring life, he had decided, was best lived
vicariously. In 1870 he published *The Ship's Career and
Other Poems*, from which the verses below are taken.

The poem, you will agree, is poignant; certainly it is
not in the least mechanistically ghoulish. The passengers,

who are no doubt surprised to find themselves sinking to a watery grave, shriek most touchingly, and the total capitulation of syntax to the overbearing necessity of rhyme, so wonderfully displayed in the last line, is heart-rending indeed.

### *From* The Loss of the Royal Charter

Friends, mourn for the loss on the dark rocky coast
Of the rough Moelfra's bay;
For shipwrecked there were the brave and fair,
Where the ship Royal Charter lay.

'Twas here the rough surges howled funeral dirges
Of sailors both hardy and brave;
And as the ship creaks heard the passengers' shrieks
As they sank to a watery grave.

They the anchor let go, 'midst confusion and woe,
To keep the ship off from the shore;
But the wind rent in twain the stout massive chain,
And we have her loss to deplore.

# William WORDSWORTH
## (1770–1850)

I need do no more than repeat Bertrand Russell's summary of Wordsworth's career: 'In his youth Wordsworth sympathized with the French Revolution, went to France, wrote good poetry, and had a natural daughter. At this period he was called a 'bad' man. Then he became 'good,' abandoned his daughter, adopted correct principles, and wrote bad poetry.'

The end of the third stanza of 'The Thorn' is deservedly famous. The lines at the end of the twelfth stanza ('It dried her body like a cinder, / And almost turn'd her brain to tinder') are just as terrible but not quite so notorious. But 'The Thorn' is not Wordsworth's worst poem; no, that honour must go to 'Ellen Irwin' – a truly awful piece of verse in which 'travelling' rhymes with 'javelin' and 'Ellen' with 'repelling'.

*From* **The Thorn**

III.

High on a mountain's highest ridge,
Where oft the stormy winter gale
Cuts like a scythe, while through the clouds
It sweeps from vale to vale,

Not five yards from the mountain-path,
This thorn you on your left espy;
And to the left, three yards beyond,
You see a little muddy pond
Of water, never dry,
I've measured it from side to side:
'Tis three feet long, and two feet wide.

VI.

Now would you see this aged thorn,
This pond and beauteous hill of moss,
You must take care and chuse your time
The mountain when to cross.
For oft there sits, between the heap
That's like an infant's grave in size,
And that same pond of which I spoke,
A woman in a scarlet cloak,
And to herself she cries,
'Oh misery! Oh misery!
'Oh woe is me! oh misery!'

VII.

At all times of the day and night
This wretched woman thither goes,
And she is known to every star,

And every wind that blows;
And there beside the thorn she sits
When the blue day-light's in the skies,
And when the whirlwind's on the hill,
Or frosty air is keen and still,
And to herself she cries,
'Oh misery! oh misery!
'Oh woe is me! oh misery!'

XI.

I'll give you the best help I can:
Before you up the mountain go,
Up to the dreary mountain-top,
I'll tell you all I know.
'Tis now some two and twenty years,
Since she (her name is Martha Ray)
Gave with a maiden's true good will
Her company to Stephen Hill;
And she was blithe and gay,
And she was happy, happy still
Whene'er she thought of Stephen Hill.

XII.

And they had fix'd the wedding-day,
The morning that must wed them both;

But Stephen to another maid
Had sworn another oath;
And with this other maid to church
Unthinking Stephen went –
Poor Martha! on that woful day
A cruel, cruel fire, they say,
Into her bones was sent:
It dried her body like a cinder,
And almost turn'd her brain to tinder.

## Ellen Irwin: or, The Braes of Kirtle

Fair Ellen Irwin, when she sat
Upon the braes of Kirtle,
Was lovely as a Grecian maid
Adorned with wreathes of myrtle;
Young Adam Bruce beside her lay,
And there did they beguile the day
With love and gentle speeches,
Beneath the budding beeches.

From many knights and many squires
The Bruce had been selected;
And Gordon, fairest of them all,
By Ellen was rejected.
Sad tidings to that noble Youth!
For it may be proclaimed with truth,

If Bruce hath loved sincerely,
That Gordon loves as dearly.

But what are Gordon's form and face,
His shattered hopes and crosses,
To them, 'mid Kirtle's pleasant braes,
Reclined on flowers and mosses?
Alas that ever he was born!
The Gordon, crouched behind a thorn,
Sees them and their caressing;
Beholds them blest and blessing.

Proud Gordon, maddened by the thoughts
That through his brain are travelling,
Rushed forth, and at the heart of Bruce
He launched a deadly javelin!
Fair Ellen saw it as it came,
And, starting up to meet the same,
Did with her body cover
The Youth, her chosen lover.

And, falling into Bruce's arms,
Thus died the beauteous Ellen,
Thus, from the heart of her true love,
The mortal spear repelling.
And Bruce, as soon as he had slain
The Gordon, sailed away to Spain;

And fought with rage incessant
Against the Moorish crescent.

But many days, and many months,
And many years ensuing,
This wretched Knight did vainly seek
The death that he was wooing.
So, coming his last help to crave,
Heart-broken, upon Ellen's grave
His body he extended,
And there his sorrow ended.

Now ye, who willingly have heard
The tale I have been telling,
May in Kirkconnell churchyard view
The grave of lonely Ellen:
By Ellen's side the Bruce is laid;
And, for the stone upon his head,
May no rude hand deface it,
And its forlorn Hic facet!

A SELECTION OF PRION HUMOUR CLASSICS:

AUGUSTUS CARP ESQ
Henry Howarth Bashford
introduced by Robert Robinson
"much funnier and darker than *Diary of a Nobody*, with which
it is often compared" *Independent on Sunday*
1-85375-411-0

SEVEN MEN AND TWO OTHERS
Max Beerbohm
introduced by Nigel Williams
"the funniest book about literature ever written" Nigel Williams
1-85375-415-3

THE FREAKS OF MAYFAIR
E F Benson
introduced by Brian Masters
"acid-tongued... peerless" *Kirkus Review*
1-85375-429 3

THE MARSH MARLOWE LETTERS
Craig Brown
introducted by Craig Brown
"I doubt there is a better parodist alive" Matthew Paris, *The
Spectator*
1-85375-461-7

DIARY OF A PROVINCIAL LADY *
E M Delafield
introduced by Jilly Cooper
"an incredibly funny social satire... the natural predecessor to
Bridget Jones" *The Times*
1-85375-368-8

A MELON FOR ECSTASY
John Fortune and John Wells
introduced by John Fortune
1-85375-470-6

THE PAPERS OF A J WENTWORTH, BA
H F Ellis
introduced by Miles Kington
"a gloriously funny account of the day-to-day life
of an earnest, humourless and largely ineffective
school master" *The Daily Mail*
1-85375-398-X

SQUIRE HAGGARD'S JOURNAL
Michael Green
introduced by the author
"marvellously funny spoof of the 18th-century
diarists" *The Times*
1-85375-399-8

THE DIARY OF A NOBODY
George and Weedon Grossmith
introduced by William Trevor
"a kind of Victorian Victor Meldrew" *The Guardian*
1-85375-364-5

THREE MEN IN A BOAT
Jerome K Jerome
introduced by Nigel Williams
"the only book I've fallen off a chair laughing at"
Vic Reeves
1-85375-371-8

THE UNSPEAKABLE SKIPTON
Pamela Hansford Johnson
introduced by Ruth Rendell
"A superb comic creation."
*The New Statesman*
1-85375-471-4

SUNSHINE SKETCHES OF A LITTLE TOWN
Stephen Leacock
introduced by Mordecai Richler
"there is no-one quite like Leacock, and no-one quite so good"
*Tatler*
1-85375-367-X

HERE'S LUCK
Lennie Lower
"Australia's funniest book" Cyril Pearl
1-85375-428-5

THE AUTOBIOGRAPHY OF A CAD
A G Macdonell
introduced by Simon Hoggart
"wonderfully sharp, clever, funny and cutting"
Simon Hoggart
1-85375-414-5

THE SERIAL *
Cyra McFadden
introduced by the author
"an American comic masterpiece" *The Spectator*
1-85375-383-1

THE UNREST-CURE AND OTHER BEASTLY TALES
Saki
introduced by Will Self
"they dazzle and delight" Graham Greene
1-85375-370-X

THE ENGLISH GENTLEMAN
Douglas Sutherland
"extremely funny" Jilly Cooper
1-85375-418-8

MY LIFE AND HARD TIMES *
James Thurber
introduced by Clifton Fadiman
"just about the best thing I ever read" Ogden Nash
1-85375-397-1

A TOUCH OF DANIEL
Peter Tinniswood
introduced by David Nobbs
"the funniest writer of his generation"
*The Times*
1-85375-463-3

CANNIBALISM IN THE CARS – THE BEST OF TWAIN'S HUMOR-
OUS SKETCHES
Mark Twain
introduced by Roy Blount Jr
"as funny now as when it was written in 1868"
*The Independent*
1-85375-369-6

* for copyright reasons these titles are not available in the USA
or Canada in the Prion edition.